HOW TO GET INTO THE
RIGHT
COLLEGE

Secrets of College
Admissions Officers

HOW TO GET INTO THE
RIGHT COLLEGE

Secrets of College Admissions Officers

By EDWARD B. FISKE
Education Columnist of *The New York Times*

with
Bruce Hammond and Amy Stuart Wells

Illustrations by Nishan Akgulian

𝕿imes BOOKS

Copyright © 1988 by Edward B. Fiske

All rights reserved under International and Pan-American Copyright Conventions. Published in the United States by Times Books, a division of Random House, Inc., New York, and simultaneously in Canada by Random House of Canada Limited, Toronto.

Library of Congress Cataloging-in-Publication Data

Fiske, Edward B.
  How to get into the right college.

  1. Universities and colleges—United States—
Admission. I. Hammond, Bruce. II. Wells, Amy Stuart.
III. Title.
LB2351.2.F57 1988 378'.1056 87-40598

ISBN 0-8129-1732-4 (pbk.)

Manufactured in the United States of America

9 8 7 6 5 4 3 2

First Edition

Design by Karin Batten

FOREWORD

As the reader will quickly gather, most of the advice in this book comes straight from the horse's mouth—from the admissions directors at the country's top colleges and universities.

Over 150 of them responded to a detailed questionnaire soliciting their advice, wisdom and reflections on their own experiences in college admissions. We appreciate their help, and would like to begin with a few observations about that most hardy species: the *directorus admissionus Americanus*.

First, and contrary to what one might expect, admissions counselors lead a surprisingly precarious life. At various times, our valiant sources have been offered bribes, seduced by parents and thrown up upon by nervous applicants. One director had his car sideswiped in a high school parking lot by a student hurrying to make it to a college interview—with him! Another told how the parent of a rejected applicant "sat calmly in my office and exclaimed that if he had a gun in his hands he would have shot me."

Other indignities are more subtle. Larry Stone of William Jewell College tells of the admissions officer who interviewed a student in his home and, as the hour grew late, was invited to stay overnight. In the middle of the night, after a quick trip to the bathroom, he found that the family dog had crawled into his bed. The counselor tried to shoo the dog off the mattress, but the dog began growling and snapping. The counselor spent the rest of the night "sleeping fitfully on the floor."

Through such trials, most American admissions directors maintain a remarkably vigorous commitment to their profession. They refuse to be slaves to numbers and take pride in seeing candidates as real live people. Their most rewarding moments, they say, come when they spot that unlikely candidate who turns out to have a successful academic career.

Thomas Rajala of American University, for example, recalls the application from a girl who had been a "medical miracle"—the first person ever born with a particular set of birth defects to be treated and survive. Her academic record and SAT scores were underwhelming, but the counselor sensed other reasons to do battle on her behalf. "Here was a girl who wasn't supposed to live, let alone walk, and she had become a dancer," he recalls. She was admitted and eventually graduated. "I'll never forget this kid," says Mr. Rajala. "She has kept me in admissions all this time."

We were impressed by the commitment of admissions directors to the broader goals of American higher education. Counselors are, by definition, gatekeepers and sorters of people. They work hard to promote the interests of their institutions in an increasingly competitive climate. But most have a commitment to higher education.

"Many of us see our roles as educators trying to assist students work through a very complicated and complex period of their lives," says David Erdmann of Rollins College. "If we can help them in some way to attain their goals—whether or not they select our institution—that seems reward enough."

We share this goal, which is why we wrote this guide and why we dedicate it to the admissions counselors who helped make it possible.

CONTENTS

HOW TO GET INTO THE
RIGHT
COLLEGE

Secrets of College
Admissions Officers

1

GETTING STARTED

Nobody ever said that applying to college would be easy.

Just ask the hapless applicant to Haverford College who was so nervous that after his interview he missed the waiting room door and instead walked into a closet. He was so embarrassed at his mistake that he just stayed there. "It was some minutes before he came out to face the room full of people staring at him," recalls Delsie Phillips, the admissions officer.

Such are the potential pitfalls of today's college applicants.

Applying to college can be an unsettling experience. People tell you that the outcome could shape the rest of your life, yet the process seems cloaked in mystery.

That's why we wrote this book—to demystify college admissions.

We went straight to the people who know best—the country's top admissions directors—and asked them the questions that are most on applicants' minds. How important is the SAT? Should you take a cram course? What should you look for when visiting a college? How do you make your essay stand out from thousands of others?

Reading this book can't guarantee a "fat" letter from Harvard or Stanford. Like anything else, getting into the college of your choice takes a lot of hard work, a lot of preparation and sometimes a little bit of luck.

But we can assure you that if you follow the tips we have picked up and dutifully passed on, you'll find a college that's just right for *you*.

Take the information provided here and go find yourself a good college. We're confident that you will.

2

THE POKER GAME

Time to ante up and cut the deck. In the 1980s, college admissions has become a nationwide poker game—with the admissions offices holding most of the aces. There are lots of good schools out there, but if you've set your sights on a selective one, you've joined a swelling cast of thousands seeking admission. How well you fare could depend on the cards:

• Maybe Dream U. will have an off year recruiting applicants from your state. You're in.

• Or maybe it'll just happen to get applications from twelve other championship rugby players just like you. You're out.

• Or maybe, just maybe, the marching band will need one more French horn player to round out its brass section. You're in.

The list of possible criteria is virtually endless. Since each class is always a little different from the last, there's no way to predict what position any one person will occupy amid the eager masses. Depending on the applicant pool, this year's admit could be next year's reject—or vice versa.

It hasn't always been this way. As recently as ten years ago, colleges pretty much accepted every applicant who was qualified. Many still do (see Chapter 3, "Designer Labels"), but these days the top schools are swamped with applications from many more academically able students than they can handle. Who's to say how they should choose among them? Would you rather admit the tennis player with the 3.50 GPA or the concert cellist with the 3.49? How many math geniuses should be admitted for every artsy dilettante? And how many polite Midwesterners should there be to balance off all the pushy New Yorkers?

Under these circumstances, it's no surprise that desperate applicants will grasp at any straw to set themselves apart from the crowd. One applicant to Stanford took out a full-page ad in the school paper begging the admissions office to admit him, while an audacious University of Virginia applicant actually sent a shoe with the message: "Now that I have one foot in the door, I hope you'll let me have the other." This little stratagem might have worked, but the other shoe dropped when nearby William and Mary received the exact same treatment— and compared notes with UVA. So much for originality.

Before you throw up your hands in despair, take heart. Though *unpredictable,* the process is far from *arbitrary.* We can't guarantee you a winning hand in the college admissions game, but we can show you how to play your cards right. In this chapter, we teach you the rules of the game and give you an inside look at both the logic that drives it and the randomness that makes it so maddeningly unpredictable. The rest of the book is devoted to how you can play the game to win.

COLLEGES VARY

The first thing to keep in mind is that not every college has applicants beating down its door. At the many hundreds of less selective and nonselective schools in the nation—and at most public universities—admissions is hardly a poker game at all. Meet the minimum standards and you're in. At the University of Wyoming, for instance, admission is guaranteed as long as you get passing marks in high school. Grades are generally the deciding factor in the highly competitive University of California system, though in this case they have to be a lot higher. The process begins to get dicey at schools that get more academically qualified applicants than they have room for. Admissions officers at the most selective of these could actually pick a second or third class from the students they reject and end up with roughly the same academic profile. Stanford University is a good example: Only about a quarter of the applicants who score over 700 on the math SAT get in. Among those with 4.0 grade point averages, the admissions rate jumps to a stratospheric 40 percent!

At such schools, the process becomes more subjective, and more like a riverboat gambling game.

What the Odds Are

Below are freshman admissions profiles for two highly selective private universities, which show the acceptance rates for students with various test scores and class ranks. Though both profiles are from particular schools, they are meant to be representative.

THE SAT

	Accepted/Denied
Over 1400	67%/33%
1200–1390	46%/53%
1000–1190	31%/69%
800–990	17%/83%
Below 800	3%/97%

As is clear from this profile of applicants to Northwestern University, getting a 1400 on the SAT (or a comparable ACT score) is no guarantee of admission at a top private college. But neither does a score below 1200 mean rejection. For anyone who scores between 1100 and 1300, the odds are about even, and the decision will depend largely on other factors, such as grades, recommendations, extracurriculars, etc.

CLASS RANK

Public Schools

Rank in Class (Percentile)	Accepted/Denied
95th or above	59%/41%
90th to 94th	27%/73%
80th to 89th	14%/86%
60th to 79th	11%/89%

40th to 59th	3%/97%
20th to 39th	2%/98%
0 to 19th	0%/100%

Private and Parochial Schools
Rank in Class (Percentile)	Accepted/Denied
95th or above	63%/37%
90th to 94th	45%/55%
80th to 89th	29%/71%
60th to 79th	19%/81%
40th to 59th	8%/92%
20th to 39th	4%/96%
0 to 19th	0%/100%

The University of Pennsylvania supplied this profile, showing acceptance rates for applicants from both public and private high schools. For those at the top of the class, it doesn't much matter which kind of school you went to. The odds for public school students tend to tail off a bit faster once they get below the top 10 percent.

WHAT THEY'RE LOOKING FOR

Cliff Sjogren of the University of Michigan sums up what most selective colleges seek: "We want a class of serious, bright, intellectually curious students that represents the many populations of our country in terms of geographical, economic, racial, ethnic, religious, and political characteristics. We seek students who pursue one or more school or nonschool activities through to levels of distinction. Special efforts are taken to enroll gifted writers, artists, athletes, musicians, as well as those with diverse interests or experience in specific areas of study."

In other words, colleges want a well-rounded CLASS—not to be confused with a bunch of well-rounded INDIVIDUALS. (See Chapter 11, "By Hook or by Crook.")

It may not matter whether you have terrific grades and are a terrific athlete and artist to boot. Any one particular strong point may be enough to distinguish you, to make you part of a well-rounded class.

WHAT'S MY CATEGORY?

Few if any admissions offices would admit to having quotas for the various "types" of students they seek, but practically all have rough guidelines for how many they want in each category. They need a certain number of "legacy" students to keep the alumni happy, a certain number of All-Americans to satisfy the athletic department, a certain number of minorities to keep the campus racially diverse, etc.

As a result, how you stack up with the other applicants in your category will go a long way toward determining your fate.

If you're not in one of the sought-after subgroups, you'll be competing directly with lots of applicants for the limited number of spots not earmarked for particular groups. In that case, it'll take some stellar academics and/or a lot of well-roundedness to get you in.

The Crap Shoot: Your Chances

Here are the approximate chances for admission for different "types" of applicants at one highly selective private college:

All applicants————1 in 3
Alumni children————1 in 2
Minority students————1 in 1.3
"Typical" applicants————1 in 7

AGAINST ALL ODDS

One special category that isn't much talked about is something that might be dubbed "the underdog factor."

Admissions officers dearly love candidates who come from underprivileged backgrounds or who have overcome great obstacles. After sifting through hordes of well-coached, well-manicured applicants, admissions officers tend to find this type of applicant refreshing.

"It is Mark from New Jersey who had dropped out of high school to work with his dad . . . or Jane, who never considered going to college until the spring of her junior year. They are why I stay in admissions," says Lynette Robinson-Weening of Simmons College.

If you fall into that category, don't let any admissions numbers intimidate you. Your special qualifications will get their due.

HOW THEY DECIDE

Most admissions offices at selective schools evaluate applications by committee. "Our Board of Admissions consists of faculty, deans and students as well as staff," explains Natalie Aharonian of Wellesley College. Prior to coming to the full committee, the applications are generally farmed out by high school or region of the country to one or more initial readers. At this stage, individual admissions officers spend an average of, say, five minutes reading each application. Many schools use a two-part rating system for academic and nonacademic factors. The science nerd with the 4.0 GPA might be a 1E—great academics, lousy extracurricular/personal—while an All-American football player who can barely read might be a 5A. The ratings help simplify the process and identify the sure "admits" and "denys."

The borderline cases, which can cause protracted haggling, are put off until the end. If your application is one of the ones in the last batch, all rating systems go by the board, and there's no telling what will decide your fate.

How adamantly will the admissions officer who interviewed you argue your case? Will you be one of the director of admissions' "wild card" admits that he saves for students rejected by the committee as a whole? What will the music professor on the committee think of the tape you submitted?

C'mon, aces!!!

3
DESIGNER LABELS

We've seen it with everything from jeans to jewelry. Now we've got college degrees with "designer labels."

Convinced that a degree from a prestigious institution is worth whatever it takes, students are beating down the doors of the most selective public and private institutions. As a result, top schools get as many as ten applications for every seat in the freshman class.

But before you break out into a cold sweat about your bleak future, consider a few facts of life:

MOST COLLEGES ARE NOT SELECTIVE

There are approximately 2,000 four-year colleges in this country, and the overwhelming majority of them accept the overwhelming majority of the students who apply.

Just look at the numbers.

A generous definition of "selective" would be a college that turns away as many applicants as it accepts. According to estimates by the College Board, no more than 10 percent of four-year colleges in this country fit into this category. Since lots of these are specialized institutions—military academies, music conservatories—the real number of colleges which are that selective is less than 100.

Apply a more stringent definition to "selective"—accepting only one in three or four—and you're talking about fewer than fifty institutions.

Selectivity of American Four-Year Colleges

Admit 15–49% of applicants———10%
Admit 50–74% of applicants———30%

Admit 75–99% of applicants————45%
Open admissions————15%

SOURCE: College Board

THE RANKS ARE THINNING

Ever since the baby boomers began picking up their diplomas in the 1960s, the number of high school graduates has been dropping. The Census Bureau says that this will continue until the mid-1990s, with the total fall-off expected to reach 40 percent in some areas of the country (like the upper Midwest and New England).

This decline has yet to result in an overall drop in college enrollment, mainly because of older students going back to school, and an increasing number of today's high school graduates opting for more education. But colleges know that declines are inevitable and are planning ahead. For some, the problem is attracting enough warm bodies. For others, the challenge is to sustain quality. (The latter is a serious matter since the number of students with above-600 SAT scores is also dropping.)

Cooking the Numbers

One of the dirty little secrets of college admissions is that selectivity can be easily manipulated. Several years ago a well-known women's college in New England was horrified to discover that it was taking four out of five applicants. So the next year it sent out a huge number of brochures and generated a lot more applications. Image problem solved.

The moral: Don't be scared away by low acceptance rates at colleges you are interested in.

The message of all this is, to paraphrase the old recruiting poster: American colleges and universities want YOU.

Unless your Reebok size is higher than your combined SAT, there are a lot of colleges ready to offer you a first-rate education. So make sure that you apply to at least a couple of these.

Then relax.

BUT, YOU SAY, "I WANT A DESIGNER LABEL ON MY DIPLOMA"

That's great. The colleges that have them tend to be the best in the country academically. Anyone with a shot at such a school should probably try.

But here, too, try to maintain some perspective.

Ask yourself *why* you are aiming at Selective Tech. Are you really after the academic rigor, social climate and other benefits that make it worth the effort and expense? Or are you (or your parents) mainly interested in sticking the right kind of decal on the back of the family station wagon? You could end up like the student who likened his time at a well-known but (for him) inappropriate campus to "serving a four-year jail term with a $60,000 fine."

There are some legitimate reasons to seek out a status institution. If you are planning to go into some fields, like investment banking or even professional football, the image of your alma mater can be pretty important. In

many more fields, coming from a status school can help you in getting your first job.

If you have a chance, take a crack at some really selective schools. But don't limit your attention to them. Realize that there are plenty of good schools out there, and that plenty of them would love to have you. Above all, don't invest a lot of emotion in being accepted by a particular one. If you find yourself getting emotional, reread Chapter 2 ("The Poker Game").

In the long run, what really counts in a college education is what you learn and how you grow as an individual. The real point is not to get in at the most prestigious college but to find the best fit for you—a school where you will feel comfortable and develop your own potential to the fullest. As John Lind of Southwestern University puts it, "It's more important to graduate than to be admitted."

4

SIZING YOURSELF UP

Perhaps the most difficult aspect of the college application process is the self-assessment part. Before you throw yourself and your life history on the mercy of college admissions officers, you need to take some time to objectively and honestly evaluate your strengths and weaknesses, likes and dislikes. What do you have to offer a college? What can the college do for you?

Unlike the high school selection process, which is usually an act of fate based on your parents' property lines, income level or religious affiliation, picking a college is a procedure you can't brush off onto dear ol' Mom and Dad. You have to take the initiative. You're the best judge of how well each school fits your personal needs and academic goals.

"If students can think of college shopping as a process of self-discovery by which they can examine their values and their sense of themselves," says Douglas Paschall of the University of the South, "then they can go off to college with less anxiety and more sensible and realistic ambitions."

What you decide about yourself translates into likes and dislikes for different kinds of institutions. Here are a few of the factors to consider when evaluating potential colleges:

ITTY-BITTY SCHOOL BLUES

If you're the type of person who thrives on individual attention and lots of it, then you're going to want to begin your search with the smaller, primarily undergraduate colleges.

It's important to realize, however, that while you will receive more attention and counseling at a smaller school, you will also miss out on some of the extras that come with a larger university—a wider variety of strong departments, better facilities and an inexhaustible supply of new people to meet. While students generally encounter less tension at small colleges—you can always find your way back to your dorm even on the first day of classes—after two or three years on the same tiny campus, you might find the atmosphere a bit confining.

ESCAPE FROM PARENTAL CONTROL

What about going far away from home? There are different ways to look at it. Some students aren't quite ready to move out of the house yet; others like to stay close enough to make an occasional road trip home for a heavy dose of Mom's lasagna.

Then there are those students who look at college as the perfect opportunity to explore new areas of the country and get as far away from any parental influence as possible. This sink-or-swim approach to gaining independence can be a particularly effective method in learning how to handle negative checking account balances, blue-jean-eating washing machines and irrational professors all by yourself. Besides, if you're lucky, Mom will send you a CARE package or two before Christmas vacation. But no lasagna.

SINGLE-SEX EDUCATION IN THE 1990s?

Before you turn up your nose at single-sex schools, you might want to listen to some of the reasons why students choose them.

Women often find single-sex schools more conducive to the development of their self-confidence and professional skills. Men who attend single-sex schools say they enjoy a feeling of camaraderie and find it easier to concentrate on their courses without women on the campus during the week.

RURAL VERSUS URBAN

Do you picture yourself spending Sunday afternoons on a grassy knoll with a thick blanket beneath you, endless blue sky above you and nothing but wide open space all around you? Or is your idea of the perfect Sunday afternoon spent in a warm and smoky coffee house in Manhattan?

A college's setting is more than a setting; it becomes a way of life for the students who go there. Some students go through withdrawal if they spend more than a few days away from city nightlife; others crave long bike rides in the country or walks along the beach.

TESTING THE ACADEMIC CLIMATE

Type A personality? Are you a go-getter, someone who welcomes and is stimulated by competition? Or do you find high-anxiety situations distasteful? You may prefer a more group-oriented, we're-all-in-this-together approach to learning.

Students come in both styles, and so do colleges. Make sure the college's intellectual climate suits your personality.

PRICE TAGS

Why would you want to go to a selective, private university that costs $18,000 a year (not including books or spending money) when you could just hike down the road to a much less expensive State U., especially if your state happens to be California, Michigan or Wisconsin? That's a very good question.

These days college is expensive no matter where you go, but some schools, and not necessarily the inferior schools, are less expensive than others. Indeed, some colleges artificially raise tuition just so they will be perceived as "better" than they are.

A smart shopper will not go to State U. or any other public school just because it's cheaper than another school that better suits his academic, social and extracurricular needs. Never take a college price tag literally. (See Chapter 22, "Footing the Bill.")

As you can see, there are going to be pros and cons to every school in the country. Your job is to figure out which pros will benefit you the most and which cons will give you the least grief. The key is to be honest with yourself, open-minded and willing to imagine yourself in several different situations.

It doesn't matter if your high school buddies think it's ignorant to consider a tiny school set in the wilds of the Northwest. It doesn't matter that half the students in your high school subscribe to the Ivy-League-or-bust philosophy. They're not you.

As Amy Harris of Scripps College points out, "You'll never regret trying something new, but you may regret a missed opportunity. Trust yourself and your instincts, but educate yourself as much as possible before relying on instincts."

5

GETTING HELP

You've got a mailbox full of admissions brochures and a slew of unanswered questions about colleges. Where are you going to turn for help? Guidance counselors? College guides? Friends? Even parents?

The answer, of course, is all of the above, though exactly who provides the best advice will depend on your circumstances. Everyone will have an opinion, and how well you sort them all out could determine the success or failure of your college search.

The first place to go for advice is almost always the high school guidance office. Ideally, your counselor will be a friend and confidant throughout the entire process, someone you can go to every few weeks to discuss and evaluate your progress. Unfortunately, most counselors are overworked, underpaid and responsible for everything from crowd control to watering the principal's plants, so don't fret if that kind of personal service isn't possible. Here are some tips on making the best of the situation:

GET TO KNOW YOUR COUNSELOR

"Start early in developing a relationship with your counselor by seeking advice on curriculum choices, activities, etc. before you begin to seek help in more pressured situations," says Teresa Lahti-Gathje of the University of Miami. *"Make yourself known!"*

Also, bear in mind that your counselor is the person who will be filling out your school recommendation form. You'll undoubtedly get a much better recommendation if he or she knows you personally. (See Chapter 19, "Getting Good Recommendations.")

DON'T EXPECT TO BE SPOON-FED

You're the one applying to college—not your counselor. The counselor should be a resource, not a High Authority.

Before your first meeting about colleges, do some homework and come prepared with a list of colleges to discuss. Then use the counselor as a sounding board about where to dig deeper: "Don't ask them to tell you about college X," says Lorna Blake of Smith College. "Ask them how/ where you can find the information."

Many counselors keep records of how past applicants from your school fared, and they should be able to give you a realistic assessment of your chances at particular schools and suggest others where students with your interests and grades have had success.

Remember also that your counselor isn't infallible. Even the best know more about some schools (especially those nearby) than others, and occasionally their perceptions will be dated or based on inaccurate information. Ask about your counselor's source of information. Whenever possible, double check what your counselor says with teachers, college guides, etc.

Give the counselor plenty of lead time before deadlines, and don't just assume that everything is done once you hand in your part of the application. "There are a myriad of horror stories of students rejected at college X because a counselor sent the wrong transcript, etc.," cautions Tom Tenges of Moravian College. "Diligent follow-up by both student and parent with the guidance counselor often can prevent that kind of foul-up."

WATCH OUT FOR THE RUNAROUND

Most counselors want only what is best for their counselees, but a few have other agendas that may run counter to your best interests.

Some counselors have pet schools, including—surprise!—their alma maters, while others are under pressure from principals or parents to steer applicants to certain "designer label" schools. Still others will try to discourage you from applying to certain colleges because "too many" students from your school are already applying there.

"Beware of the guidance counselors who attempt to restrict options by giving such advice as: it's too costly or too far away; no one I know goes there; it's not right for you. A good guidance counselor will expand horizons and help find information," says Richard Hallin of Eckerd College.

HIGH-PRICED ADVICE

Depending on how good your school's guidance department is, you may want to consider a private counselor. It'll cost you a fair piece of change—from a few hundred dollars up to $2,000 for a full admissions process package—but it could be worth it if you can't get good advice from your school. These services range from helping you draw up a list to advice on test-taking, filling out applications, writing essays and managing acceptances and wait-listing.

Just don't sign on under the illusion that an independent counselor will somehow get you in through inside connections or "pulling strings." If you can't stand on your own qualifications, no amount of high-priced consulting and packaging will make any difference.

EVEN MOM AND DAD CAN HELP

Aside from professional counselors, your most important source of information in the admissions process could well be your parents. They know you better than anyone.

A lot will depend on your past relationship with your parents, but in general it is best to avoid the extremes of relying exclusively on them or locking them out of the process altogether. Try to settle on some ground rules from the beginning as to how much they are willing to pay, how much input they will have in the final choice, etc. An understanding early in the process could prevent a lot of heartache and bitterness over a disagreement at the end.

FRIENDS AND TEACHERS, TOO

Older friends at colleges you are considering can also be a fertile source of information, so long as you keep in mind that the same student who sings his school's praises during spring break may curse it up and down if you happen to catch him during exams. Ask your counselor for a list of everyone from your school who attends the colleges you're interested in, and don't be shy about contacting them. If there are any teachers you respect and who know you well, by all means ask if they have any schools to recommend.

COLLEGE GUIDES

A final source you should definitely consult are college guides, which come in two basic types. First are the statistical guides, which typically include hundreds of colleges and offer at best a bare-bones outline of key facts about academic life. Meatier and more interesting are the subjective guides, which offer essays with critical evaluations of each school. A bibliography can be found in the next chapter.

WHAT ARE YOU WAITING FOR?

Though all the sources we've mentioned here should prove useful, none by itself holds the key to a successful college search. In the end, there is really no substitute for persistence and critical thinking, both in seeking out sources of information and in piecing the bits of advice into a coherent whole. If you really want your college search to be a success, it will be. All you have to do is roll up your sleeves and get to work.

6

RECOMMENDED READING

COLLEGE GUIDES

Fiske, Edward B., FISKE GUIDE TO COLLEGES, Times Books. Includes critical essays on 295 of the most selective colleges and universities in the nation. A good place to begin the college search for applicants interested in selective colleges.

Fiske, Edward B., and Joseph Michalak, THE BEST BUYS IN COLLEGE EDUCATION, Times Books. A guide for the cost-conscious applicant who doesn't want to sacrifice quality. Includes articles on over 200 "bargain" schools.

Yale Daily News, THE INSIDER'S GUIDE TO THE COLLEGES, St. Martin's Press. Covers the most prominent schools in a format similar to the *Fiske Guide.* Useful for comparisons.

Hegener, Karen C., THE COMPETITIVE COLLEGES, Peterson's Guides. The best statistical guide to selective colleges. Offers detailed profiles of over 300 schools.

Cass, James, and Max Birnbaum, COMPARATIVE GUIDE TO AMERICAN COLLEGES, Harper & Row. A comprehensive guide that mixes statistics and prose descriptions. Good for applicants who aren't sure whether they want to go to a selective or nonselective school.

Lehman, Andrea E., ed., GUIDE TO FOUR-YEAR COLLEGES 1988, Peterson's Guides. Contains statistical profiles of over 1,900 schools.

FINANCIAL AID

Cassidy, David J., and Michael J. Alves, THE SCHOLARSHIP BOOK: THE COMPLETE GUIDE TO PRIVATE-SECTOR SCHOLARSHIPS, GRANTS, AND

LOANS FOR UNDERGRADUATES, Prentice-Hall. A listing of over 50,000 scholarships. Includes information on who can apply, what the criteria are, and where to write.

College Scholarship Service, THE COLLEGE COST BOOK, The College Entrance Examination Board. Includes a breakdown of expenses at approximately 3,500 two- and four-year schools. Includes advice for estimating college costs and general information about finding aid. Published by the same group that prepares the Financial Aid Form (FAF).

Deutschman, Alan, WINNING MONEY FOR COLLEGE, Peterson's Guides. Information on over 50 of the most prominent national scholarship contests. Good for students who are especially gifted in a particular school subject, or have special talent in areas such as creative writing, painting, music, etc.

Hegener, Karen C., THE COLLEGE MONEY HANDBOOK, Peterson's Guides. Offers a detailed description of costs and scholarship opportunities at 1,700 four-year schools. Also provides general information about getting money for college.

Leider, Robert, and Anna Leider, DON'T MISS OUT: THE AMBITIOUS STUDENT'S GUIDE TO FINANCIAL AID, Octameron Associates. A comprehensive guide that gives a concise summary of the essentials of financial aid. A good source of practical information on financial strategies and names and addresses of people to write.

THE SAT

There are literally dozens of books on how to prepare for, beat, ace, and/or psyche out the SAT. These generally fall into one of two categories:

- The old reliable models, which include vocabulary lists, equation reviews, and practice tests.
- The racy new variety that focuses on out-thinking the test-maker and "beating the system."

In general, we recommend the former. But if you find one with a gimmick that works for you, there's no reason not to get it. Just be sure that the book you buy includes some practice problems that give you an idea of what to expect on the test.

The standard manuals are all pretty much the same; any one of them will prepare you for the test. How useful they are is really a function of how hard you are willing to work. We do, however, recommend *SAT Success*, written by Joan Davenport Carris and published by Peterson's Guides. This is the only book that offers different plans depending on how much time you have to prepare.

THE ACT, ACHIEVEMENT TESTS, AND AP TESTS

The guides to these tests are fewer in number and basically all the same. They offer a review of the relevant material and some practice problems and/or tests. Simply scout out a couple of bookstores in your area and buy whichever one(s) looks best to you.

For an overview of the Achievement Tests, you may want to consider *The College Board Achievement Tests: 14 Tests in 13 Subjects,* published by the College Board, which includes one sample test in each subject. This book will be particularly valuable for students who haven't decided which Achievement Tests to take and want to see how well they are prepared in one or more subjects.

7

SHAPING
THE TRANSCRIPT

High school transcripts tell it all—the good, the bad and the ugly. That's why admissions directors will consider your transcript the key ingredient to their evaluation of your potential success as a college student. "The transcript is a four-year record of performance," says Daniel Walls of Emory University. "It can't be coached."

The minute admissions committees get hold of your transcript, they scrutinize it, snooping for every tidbit of information. They look for EVERYTHING, from the most obvious—courses taken, grade-point average, grade patterns, class rank—to the less obvious, i.e., organizational skills, work habits, attendance patterns and motivation.

How can they possibly derive so much personal information from a few measly pieces of paper? Let's look at two examples:

THE RISE AND FALL OF TWO STUDENTS

Meet Alfred and Bernadette. Alfred only had so-so grades in ninth grade but has been improving steadily ever since. As his grades went up, he began to take more and more challenging high school courses. His transcript tells the admissions committee that he learned to take his education more seriously.

Now for Bernadette. Her transcript portrays a strong academic record in the ninth grade followed by a slither into mediocrity during the subsequent years. This pattern of achievement communicates an increasingly less motivated attitude that admissions committees will want to avoid.

The conclusion? Even if Alfred has a slightly lower overall GPA and class rank, he would most likely be the preferred candidate at many schools.

. . .

Still, there are other ways to impress or turn off admissions committees. Here's another scenario:

HOW STRETCHING CAN HELP

Her name is Queeny, and she has taken a wide range of disciplines during her high school career, fearless even in the face of her worst subjects. Every year she enrolled in several Advanced Placement (AP) courses in both her favorite subjects—math and science—and her least favorite subjects—English and history—because she knew she was capable of honors-level work, and she wanted a challenge. Although her overall GPA does not place her at the top of the class, she has a solid record of having taken the most difficult courses her high school offered.

Now Rocky is a different story. He's a fun-loving kind of guy who is just as academically capable as Queeny, but he chose to take the easiest possible route to a high school diploma. His transcript is overcrowded with less-than-challenging, semi-academic courses such as "Physical Education for the 1990s: Getting a Head Start on the Battle of the Bulge." Nevertheless, Rocky has a 4.0 GPA and is ranked near the top of his class.

However, Queeny, with her lower GPA and class rank, wins more admits to selective colleges than Rocky.

Admissions committees can read between the lines of a high school transcript. They know that no one twisted your arm and made you take three study halls instead of physics and another history course your senior year.

That's why admissions people attempt to predict your college performance and motivation level by looking at both your grades and the difficulty of the courses you've taken in high school. "So-called gut courses taken to fatten a grade average are easy to spot as cosmetic transcript decoration and equally easy to discount," says George Stoner of George Washington University.

BETTER LATE THAN NEVER

Don't think your senior year is too late to do anything about a sorry transcript. If you're entering your last year of high school and haven't taken any AP courses yet, enroll now.

Another increasingly popular tactic is to sign up for one of the precollege summer school courses at an Ivy League college the summer before your senior year. A strong performance in one of these classes followed by an impressive senior year of AP courses will say a lot about your direction and determination.

TO AP OR NOT TO AP?

How many and what kind of AP courses should you take to avoid a wimpy-looking transcript? That depends on three factors:

- The type of school you're planning to apply to. Okay, the most selective schools will settle for nothing short of excellent grades in the toughest courses. But at many highly reputable but slightly less competitive colleges, lower grades in the more difficult courses beat straight As in blow-off classes. "We are generally more impressed by a B or even a C in an honors or AP course than an A in a general-level one," says Olga Euben of Hampshire College. "We respect students who are willing to take on such a challenge, even at the risk of lowering their grade-point average or rank in class."

However, keep in mind that at some large universities with more than 10,000 students, applications are initially shuffled into "acceptable" and "not acceptable" piles based on statistics. Penn State's Scott Healy admits, "Although Penn State takes honors course work into consideration, this consideration comes after the high school grade-point average and SAT scores in terms of importance."

• Your own academic strengths and weaknesses. It's important to assess your academic strengths and weaknesses before loading your schedule with advanced courses in every subject. Admissions people contend that there is such a thing as AP overload, and once your grades drop below C level, few colleges are going to care what type of courses you took.

• The AP policies at your school. Check out all the levels of courses offered at your high school and how they are distinguished from one another on transcripts. While some high schools don't even offer AP classes, others not only have a wide variety of these courses; they even "weigh" AP grades to give students extra credit for taking the tougher route. If you're going to take AP classes, make sure the additional time and effort you'll be putting into them is clearly communicated to the college admissions committee—if not on the transcript, then in letters of recommendation or in your portion of the application.

THE BOTTOM LINE?

Take the most advanced courses available in your strongest subjects. Then choose additional AP classes based on your past record in other subjects and your ability to perform well in a number of areas at once. Whatever you do, you don't want to give the impression that you skated through high school and hope to do the same in college.

"We look for energy and ambition," says James Hendrix of Davidson College. "We look for those students who have taken risks and have stretched themselves intellectually and socially and politically by virtue of the courses they have chosen."

Minimum High School Requirements for College-Bound Students

English—4 years
Math—3 years
Natural sciences—3 years
Social sciences—3 years
Foreign languages—2 years

SOURCE: College Board.

8

CUTTING THROUGH
THE PROPAGANDA

If you're wondering why Joe Admissions Officer from Most Popular University—which you've never heard of before—sent you a warm, personal letter and a slick, multicolored brochure that reads "Uncle Joe wants YOU to go to Most Popular U.," chalk it up to what Thomas Pollard of the University of Richmond calls "the mass-marketing mania." The truth is, Uncle Joe wants you—and the 100,000 or so other prospective students who also received his letter.

Since the pool of college-age students began shrinking in the early 1980s, college student recruitment programs have been kicked into high gear. Even prestigious institutions, which used to just let the applications pour in, have adopted aggressive strategies. Their need has spawned an entire industry of higher education advertising. Your mailbox is their direct pipeline.

With so much promoting going on, you're bound to get confused about what literature offers legitimate information and what's just fluffy propaganda. After about the first hundred "personal" letters, you might be tempted to pitch everything into the wastebasket. But before you start indiscriminately discarding your mail, you might want to learn how to use the promotional literature to your advantage.

WHERE IT COMES FROM

When you take the PSAT, SAT, ACT or Advanced Placement Tests, you'll fill out a registration form, and one of the questions on that form will ask if you want to receive a "free service"—the Student Search Service for the PSAT, SAT and AP Tests or the Educational Opportunity Service for the ACT.

The SAT box looks like this:

Item 8 on the Student Search Service is reproduced from the 1988–89 *Admissions Testing Program Registration Form and Student Descriptive Questionnaire,* copyright © 1988 by College Entrance Examination Board and Educational Testing Service.

8	**STUDENT SEARCH SERVICE**

For more information about the Student Search Service, see your *Registration Bulletin.*

◯ Yes, I want the College Board to send information about me to colleges, universities, and governmental scholarship programs interested in students like me.

◯ No, I do not want the College Board to send information about me to colleges, universities, and governmental scholarship programs through the Student Search Service.

What should you do? Check "Yes" and buy yourself a sturdy trash can.

"Yes" means you have authorized the administrator of that test to sell your name, address, test scores and the personal information you provided on the registration form to any college admissions office that wants to buy it. The trash can is for about 80 percent of the mail you'll get from them.

Colleges purchase lists of names of the students who fall into the specific "target" categories broken down by:

> *test scores*
> *parental income*
> *fancy zip codes*
> *intended major*
> *ethnic or religious background*
> *high school grade-point average*
> *interest in ROTC, etc.*

The list includes almost everything except sexual preference and voter registration.

The College Board's Student Search Service, the larger of the two test organizations' services, sold 40 million names to 1,100 colleges in 1986. Each college was charged $150 per search and an additional fifteen cents per name produced by that search. The Student Search annual revenues are more than $1.5 million.

BE FLATTERED

Obviously, the colleges that send you information don't just pick your name out of a phone book. They've made a large investment in courting you via the U.S. Postal Service. That's why Hayden Schilling of the College of Wooster advises students to "be patient, tolerant and realize that the mail 'deluge' represents an interest in you."

And while you shouldn't consider promotional literature an invitation to attend, keep in mind that most colleges don't waste their money on students who don't fit their profiles. With a pair of 350s on the SAT you won't be hearing from Yale.

HOW TO DEAL WITH IT

So, it turns out that 300-plus colleges are interested in you. How do you deal with all those brochures and view books?

The first thing to do is to set your priorities. Define your parameters of schools you are interested in—size, location, public or private, etc.—and then use them to divide the mail into Good, Maybe and No Way piles.

Then follow these principles:

- Read information from schools you've never heard of if they appear to offer what you're looking for.
- If it doesn't fit your needs, put literature from even the most popular schools in your newly acquired trash can.
- Use the literature to help you look beyond the obvious and broaden your search horizons.

DETECTING PUFF AND ORDERING MORE STUFF

Once you have assembled your stack of literature to peruse, begin reviewing it with a critical eye. Or, as one admissions director explained it, develop your "puffery detector." Tim Rinehart of the University of Massachusetts at Amherst recommends you get past the "ponds, swans and campus couples" stuff and get down to the nitty-gritty:

- What are the two or three basic points this college is trying to make?
- What does this college want me to know about it?

Look for a business reply card or an order form in the material you've received. If you don't find anything, give the admissions office a call and tell them you want a catalog and any other helpful material they have. But beware: Any show of interest triggers lots more information from the computer that controls the whole process.

Something else to look for amid all the literature is a description of the college's purpose, which often contains a set of criteria and can be revealing. Also, notice little things like personally signed letters. They're much nicer than the laser-printed closing, "Sincerely, The Admissions Office." How sincere can a computer be?

HOW TO READ A COLLEGE CATALOG

You might want to get your hands on a college catalog, the official document of the school. That's where you'll find more facts and less fluff per ounce. But because catalogs are big, bulky and expensive to print and mail, colleges usually reserve them for the serious prospects who request them. If that's you, get one.

Look at how the catalog is divided into sections and

how much space is allocated to various disciplines or majors. This gives you an idea of the college's academic layout. For example, is there a separate department of political science or are all poli sci majors incorporated into the school of arts and sciences?

- Read the short bios of the faculty members. Do they all have their Ph.D.s? Did they earn them at credible institutions? Does each department have a good mix of faculty who specialize in different areas of the field?
- Find the section that discusses freshmen requirements and what year students declare their majors.
- Examine the fact sheet, the page that lists total enrollment, undergrad enrollment, percentage of students receiving financial aid, etc.
- Skim through the history of the college. How long has it been around? Who founded it and why was it founded? In what ways has it grown?

9

LIES, DAMNED LIES AND STATISTICS

There are three kinds of lies: lies, DAMNED lies and statistics.
—*British Prime Minister Benjamin Disraeli*

No one likes to be called a liar, especially those at institutions committed to the pursuit of truth. But you may have noticed that flashing favorable statistics—student-faculty ratios, freshman SAT scores, etc.—in front of prospective students has become a popular college recruitment tactic.

"Either statistics say what we want or we make them come close to it," says Patricia Burgh of Seton Hall University.

But there are some ways in which you, a mild-mannered high school student, can win the battle against statistical jargon so that truth and justice might prevail in your analysis of a college. Following are some basic rules of thumb:

MEDIAN TEST SCORES AREN'T CUTOFFS

Perhaps the most common mistake made by applicants is to view "median" or "average" freshman SAT scores as cutoffs. If a college says that last year's freshmen had median scores of 500 on the verbal section and you have only 480, the temptation is to think that you don't have a shot at that institution.

Think again.

Median scores tell you where the middle of the class fell. In the instance above, half of the class had scores above 500 while half scored below that figure. Obviously many of them came in with 480s just like you.

For a more accurate sense of where you fit in look at the range of scores that encompass the middle half of the class—from the 25th to the 75th percentile. In general, this figure will range 40–50 points on either side of the median score. For example, if the median is 500, then the middle half of the freshman class will have scores between 450 and 550.

If your score is above the figure for the 75th percentile, you can assume that you will be academically comfortable at that institution—and you may want to consider a more challenging place. If your score is below that of the 25th percentile, you should expect a good deal of academic stimulation—maybe too much.

WHOM ARE THEY TALKING ABOUT ANYWAY?

Be wary about comparing colleges on the basis of average test scores. Different colleges calculate them differently.

Some institutions, when they publish "median freshman SAT scores," mean just that—the median score of all freshmen. Others, however, exclude "special admits"—athletes, children of alumni, disadvantaged students and others who are admitted under relaxed standards. Obviously the latter approach will produce a higher median score than the former.

As an applicant, you are interested in the scores of those whom you will be competing against, so it is important to understand which approach a college uses—especially if you are at the low end of the range. Let's assume that your score is at the 25th percentile of a particular college. If that institution excludes special admits in calculating the median SAT scores, then you are on pretty safe ground as far as test scores are concerned. If that figure includes all students, though, then you can assume that a substantial proportion of those in the bottom quartile are being admitted under rules that do not apply to you and thus your chances of being admitted are much lower.

NOT THE STUDENT–FACULTY RATIO AGAIN

Watch out for the "student–faculty" ratios, another all-time favorite misleading college statistic.

If a college claims to have a student–faculty ratio of 19:1, don't assume that most of your classes will only have nineteen students in them. There may be nineteen student bodies for every one adult on campus who teaches at least one course. But remember, students take four or five courses a semester while each faculty member only teaches two or three.

At large universities, "faculty" might include everyone from an adjunct business instructor, who works on Wall Street and teaches one M.B.A. class, to medical and law school profs. Small liberal arts colleges that don't have graduate programs are usually the most trustworthy on the student–faculty ratio question. A better question is "What's the average freshman class size?" (See Chapter 16, "Surviving the Interview.") Find out the ratio of professors who teach freshman courses to the number of freshmen. That's your student–faculty ratio.

NOTHING FROM NOTHING LEAVES NOTHING

Just as dubious as averages and ratios are percentages. Always ask, "percentage of what?" When a college claims that 80 percent of its graduates who applied to medical and law schools were accepted, you should immediately wonder how many applied. If only five students applied, so what? You also want to know how many got into their first-choice school, and is this a four- or five-year average or a one-shot deal?

Even worse is the college that claims, "100 percent of those students recommended by faculty members are accepted to medical schools." What sort of preselection of undergraduates takes place in the pre-med department?

Many colleges weed out unpromising applicants so their acceptance rates will be higher.

Also, beware of schools that tell you the percentage of students who receive financial aid. If this statistic isn't qualified, you have no idea how many students receive scholarships and how many have work-study jobs. And watch out for anyone who tells you that 80 percent of students *interviewed* said that the dormitories are the best in the world. How many students were surveyed? Only those living in the spiffy new campus condominiums, perhaps?

Percentage of Ph.D.s on the faculty can be another deceptive statistic. Does it really matter that 92 percent have doctorate degrees if you're being taught by the other 8 percent? Try to find out how many freshman courses are taught by graduate students and how many are taught by full professors.

AN APPLICANT CANNOT LIVE ON STATISTICS ALONE

A word of warning from Anne Price of Lewis and Clark College: "Don't judge colleges by statistics any more than you want to be judged by statistics." And because different schools calculate their stats differently, you should never use them to compare two colleges. If a particular stat is important to you, use it. But find out from the admissions offices how they are determined at each school.

As Michael Behnke of MIT advises, "Figure out what question you're trying to get answered by looking at the statistics. Then ask that question and forget the statistics."

10

SHOULD I BE AN EARLY BIRD?

The reality of college admissions can be summed up in a single phrase: The *waiting* is the hardest part.

Faced with the prospect of up to five months of nailbiting before the April 15 decision day, you may want to consider applying via an Early Decision or Early Action plan, and thereby get word of your acceptance or denial as early as December. But proceed with care. The long-term benefits of applying early are marginal, and a hasty decision can bring an abrupt end to your college search and send you packing to a less-than-ideal school.

The key point to get straight is the difference between Early Decision and Early Action. Both require a candidate to file early—generally by November—but beyond that the obligations and benefits vary.

EARLY DECISION

The Die Is Cast. Early Decision is just that—a decision. You can apply Early Decision to only one school, and if it accepts you (usually by January), you must withdraw all other applications and enroll. No ifs, ands or buts.

That's just the way the colleges like it. Early Decision allows them to assemble the makings of a class early in the admissions year. Since in the normal course of things colleges never know exactly how many of the students they accept will actually enroll, firm commitments early allow them to reduce significantly their margin of error and not end up renting out hotel rooms to handle an unexpected overflow of freshmen.

Till Death—or Graduation—Do You Part. From the moment you mail the application, there's no turning back. If accepted, you enroll. If you try to wriggle out of an Early Decision commitment, you'll surely excite the wrath of the jilted college, which could conceivably locate your new suitor school and inform it of your shenanigans, with the end result that both colleges rescind their offers.

In other words, Early Decision may give you peace of mind now, but if it comes at the expense of four years at the wrong college, it's definitely not worth it. Stirling Huntley of Cal Tech says he recommends that applicants apply Early Decision "only rarely and when he or she is absolutely convinced that our institution is the first choice based on a thorough study."

And beware. Some colleges, hungry for warm bodies to fill empty classrooms, give applicants the hard sell with Early Decision sales pitches that "come close to a form of entrapment," says Michael Behnke of MIT.

Fringe Benefits of E.D. Despite all the caveats, if you really do have a foolproof, ironclad, cross-your-heart-and-hope-to-die first choice, Early Decision could be the way to go. In addition to cutting short the suspense, there are other side benefits.

Some schools give Early Decision students a better financial aid deal. Hampden-Sydney, for example, funds Early Decision applicants at 100 percent of their financial need and everyone else at 90 percent. Other colleges, notably Connecticut College and the University of Rochester, say they give preference in admissions to Early Decision applicants.

Hayden Schilling of the College of Wooster says that Early Decision may sometimes be desirable for the "iffy" student who has set his sights on a particular college. "Colleges do consider the 'loyalty' factor," he says, "and this student may possibly enhance his/her chances of admission through Early Decision."

Take note, however, that the loyalty factor matters much less at highly selective schools that are swamped with more qualified applicants who are eager to attend than seats in the class. At these schools, the Early Decision applicant pool is often even more competitive than the regular one, and admission is no easier.

What If I Am Rejected or Deferred? Don't panic. If you're rejected at a school to which you applied Early Decision or Early Action, the process goes on as before. Keep filing those applications. If you're deferred, it means you're on the borderline—not a clear-cut admit, but definitely qualified. Your application will be considered without prejudice with the regular decision applicants, and you will be notified of a decision in April. And bear in mind that Early Decision applicants who are deferred are released from their commitment to attend if accepted.

EARLY ACTION

While applying Early Decision is a serious step, Early Action requires much less agonizing. If you have a first choice that offers Early Action, and you feel that you are a strong candidate, you might as well take the plunge.

Early Action is most often associated with four Ivy League schools—Harvard, Yale, Brown and Princeton—plus MIT, which were among the first to offer it. All of them admit a substantial percentage of their classes from the early pool.

All the Fun with No Commitment. The benefits of Early Action for the college are much the same as those of Early Decision.

The program allows the schools to get much of their admissions work out of the way by January, and though there is no commitment to attend, Early Action is generally offered at top colleges that have no trouble getting students to sign on the dotted line. These colleges can afford to give applicants more leeway and still have a good idea of how many will show up in the fall.

Tough Competition. Be forewarned: Applying Early Action rarely improves your chances, and at prestigious schools like these, competition is FIERCE. If there is any chance that your credentials will improve during the first semester of your senior year, it is best not to apply early to these or any other schools.

And keep in mind, both Early Decision and Early Action usually require you to take the SAT or ACT by June at the end of your junior year. The bottom line? START EARLY.

Timetable for Early Decision and Early Action

JUNIOR YEAR

May-June: Take SAT or ACT.

SENIOR YEAR

September-October: Work on applications. Hand out recommendation forms. Take ACT if necessary.

November: File Early Decision/Action applications according to deadlines. Follow up with recommendations. Continue working on regular decision applications. Continue taking SAT, ACT, and Achievement Tests.

December-February: Receive notification. If you are accepted Early Decision, you MUST withdraw all other applications.

A final option you may want to consider is Early Admission after your junior year of high school, offered by many schools on an ad hoc basis. If you have an outstanding record, and can offer a compelling reason why another year of high school isn't for you, many fine schools will offer you admission.

11

BY HOOK
OR BY CROOK

You keep hearing it from everyone—your nosy next-door neighbor, guidebooks, counselors—you gotta have a "hook," some special talent, some marketable quality that will make you stand out.

But it's not that easy and it's not that essential. So don't lose any sleep conjuring up a superfluous image of yourself and your never-ending list of talents. Admissions people are veteran fluff detectors. Nothing turns them off quicker than a fabricated image. When it comes to hooks, either you've got one or you don't.

TWO BRANDS OF HOOKS

Hooks come in two standard varieties: the built-in and the built-up.

The built-in is more subtle. So subtle in fact, you may have one and not even know it. You, yes you, could be the passive owner of a specific trait a college is seeking. For instance, if one of your parents or an older sibling attended a college you are applying to, chances are that school will give your application a longer look.

Your home address could be another built-in hook. If you're from a distant region or foreign country, a college that relishes its geographic mix of students will appreciate you more. If two students have identical records, the one from Montana may have a better shot at getting into Princeton than one from New York City. If racial and ethnic diversity are important to a college, applicants of underrepresented minority or religious groups will gain an immediate edge.

Of course, built-up or acquired hooks are not arrived at so passively. They are the fruits of years of sweat and toil. If you're a talented and dedicated athlete, artist or musician, you definitely want to let the admissions committee know about it. Admissions counselors tell of some interesting and impressive addenda to applications:

- portfolios of artwork
- tapes of music written or played
- photographs that illustrated a hobby
- anything that effectively depicts REAL talent and dedication.

One particularly impressive Rollins College applicant brought his bagpipes to an interview and played them for the staff in the parking lot.

An Earlham College applicant intrigued the admissions committee with a videotape of his pieces of sculpture carefully arranged in his backyard. In the tape, he described the significance of each piece and ended the tape with a shot from his roof, giving the committee a bird's-eye view of his sculpture garden.

Participation in a community or school activity or entrepreneurial ventures constitutes another category of a built-up hook. But a list of twenty clubs that you belonged to for an average of two months portrays little more than a half-hearted, insincere approach to extra-curricular activities. "The sort of hook that matters is an in-depth, self-stretching commitment of a student to a particular goal, project or cause," explains James Holmes of Washington College.

Mention of an unusual but altruistic activity that admissions directors haven't already seen a thousand times will draw additional interest. One MIT applicant who had worked with deaf children stood out when she brought to her interview a tape of herself singing and playing a song that she had written. While the tape played, she confidently "signed" the words to the song.

IF YOU'RE NOT CLEVELAND'S ANSWER TO MICHELANGELO

Now that you have an idea of what a hook is, you want to know what you should do if you don't have one.

The answer is: nothing.

College admissions people realize that not everyone can play the bagpipes or tap dance. Some say the hype about hooks is overaccentuated. "Special talents always help," says Linda Davis of Amherst College, "but there is no substitute for top intellectual power and performance." Also, a lot depends on the school and the applicant. Here are two situations in which a hook could possibly make a difference:

• At a highly competitive university where you're up against thousands of applicants with virtually flawless academic backgrounds and test scores, you're going to need more than just another pretty transcript to capture the admissions committee's attention.

• At a slightly less selective school, a hook could come in handy if you're one of those borderline cases with average academic achievement.

Other times, it won't matter if you can play five instruments, do a belly dance and chew gum all at the same time; you're either in or out based on your academic credentials. As Natalie Aharonian of Wellesley College points out, "A hook will not conceal or compensate for a lack of solid achievement." And just remember, a manufactured, phony-looking hook is worse than no hook at all.

12

HOW IMPORTANT IS THE SAT?

The SAT casts a long shadow over the selective college admissions process. To hear some people tell it, the SAT is the be-all and end-all of everything: the deciding factor on whether you get into a good school and the litmus test of your worth as an individual. "What did you get on the SAT?" will be the all-important question from test day forward, and when you die, your scores will be etched forevermore on your tombstone.

Or will they?

Is the SAT really as important as everyone seems to think? The answer—as unsatisfactory as this may sound—is "yes and no." The SAT is important, but excessive hype has blown it all out of proportion. As David Erdmann of Rollins College puts it, "At most institutions standardized test scores count less than students think and more than the colleges are willing to admit."

A NUMBER FOR YOUR THOUGHTS

The allure of using standardized tests to measure academic ability is easy to understand. They provide a simple way of making comparisons among students. No matter what high school you go to, or what courses you take, the standardized tests put you on the same scale as millions of other students after three short hours of blackening ovals with a number-two pencil. The SAT in particular has gained currency for two reasons:

• The SAT is the only standardized test that purports to measure overall academic aptitude, or what the College Board now calls "developed ability." The ACT and Achievement Tests are tied more closely to the content of specific subjects.

• The vast majority of highly selective schools require the SAT. The ACT is used mainly by southern and western state universities, though many schools will accept either the SAT or the ACT.

SAT/ACT Conversion Chart

Here is how scores on one correlate to the other, according to the people who make the SAT and the ACT. If you get a 23 on the ACT, for example, that's roughly the same as getting a 1030 on the SAT, and vice versa.

ACT	SAT		ACT	SAT
1	———		20	910
2	———		21	950
3	———		22	990
4	———		23	1030
5	———		24	1070
6	———		25	1110
7	———		26	1150
8	430		27	1190
9	470		28	1230
10	510		29	1270
11	550		30	1310
12	590		31	1350
13	630		32	1390
14	670		33	1430
15	710		34	1470
16	750		35	1510
17	790		36	1550
18	830		———	1600
19	870			

SOURCE: Educational Testing Service and American College Testing Program.

PROBLEM? DID SOMEONE SAY PROBLEM?

Back about World War II, people really believed that you could measure intelligence and put a single number on it. Nobody believes that anymore, but the SAT—which developed out of that notion—lives on.

Meanwhile, studies have shown that the high school transcript is a better predictor of academic performance than standardized tests. As Roy Nelson of Bryant College notes, "You just cannot equate three years of high school with one three-hour exam on a Saturday morning."

There is also growing suspicion that standardized tests—notably the SAT—are discriminatory on the basis of race, sex and socioeconomic background.

Finally, there is the realization that it is possible to increase scores on the SAT through private coaching. With SAT prep courses a burgeoning industry, many observers believe that part of what it measures is how well students have been drilled to take a particular kind of test. (See Chapter 13, "To Cram or Not to Cram?")

But all this brings us back to where we started. How important is the SAT? Answer: It varies from college to college, depending on where they stand in the debate outlined above.

How Accurate Are SAT Scores?

Not very.

Testmakers don't exactly shout it from the hills, but when pressed they concede that standardized admissions tests are far from precise.

Take your SAT score, for example. There's one chance in *three* that the 550 that arrived in the little envelope from ETS should really be at least 580 or no more than 520. There's one chance in *ten* that it should be either in the low 600s or the high 400s.

Here's why.

The SAT can't measure everything that you know (like

your entire vocabulary) in one Saturday morning. So by necessity every test is a *sample* of your academic knowledge and ability, and the nature of this sample varies with every edition of the test. The result, for purely statistical reasons, is what is known as the "standard error of measurement" (SEM).

The SEM on the SAT is 30 points. Since roughly one million students take the SAT every year, this means that about 335,000 reported scores are off by at least 30 points, and 100,000 are off by at least 60 points. And this doesn't take into account subjective influences such as the fact that you may have arrived at the test site with a headache.

The margin of error can be illustrated graphically. Suppose 60 students have reported scores of 580. According to the laws of statistics, their "true" scores will break down as follows:

520 or below	520–550	550–580	580–610	610–640	640 or above
3	7	20	20	7	3

College admissions officers—at least the good ones—understand this. That's why they don't pay much attention to score differentials of 30 or 40 points.

Neither should you.

WHERE THE SAT HAS CLOUT

The group that generally puts the most emphasis on the SAT is large state universities. Many such schools must accept all "qualified" in-state applicants, and the easiest way to accomplish that mandate is to use SAT and grade-point cutoffs. Scores typically make up a fourth to a half of the "acceptance formulas" at these schools.

A second category of schools where the SAT and other

standardized tests carry a lot of weight is technical institutes. "At a highly selective institution of engineering, math and science scores must be within certain ranges in order for a student to be competitive," says Duncan Murdoch of Harvey Mudd College. Stirling Huntley of Cal Tech says that test scores are "frequently the deciding factor" in admissions decisions.

WHERE IT DOESN'T

At the opposite end of the spectrum are schools that have stopped requiring the SAT altogether. The staunchest anti-test institutions tend to be liberal arts colleges with a slightly alternative approach to education. Small but selective Hampshire College, for instance, requires no tests at all. "Quite simply," explains Olga Euben, "we do not think that performance on a multiple-choice test is an accurate predictor of how students will perform in Hampshire's individualized academic program."

More mainstream liberal arts colleges generally require tests but are apt to put more emphasis on things like grades and the essay. A seat-of-the-pants generalization: the smaller the school, the less standardized test scores are likely to matter.

Selective Schools That Don't Require the SAT or ACT

Bates College
Bradford College
Bowdoin College
Hampshire College
Middlebury College
Union College
Ursinus College

THE GREAT MIDDLE

Finally, there is the great middle: schools where standardized test scores are important, but not that important.
Or something like that.

At most colleges, test scores are one of a range of factors
used in making admissions decisions. Rarely are they as
critical as the transcript. Indeed, test scores tend to become a factor only when they are out of sync with the
grade point average. Low SAT scores are a red flag to look
more closely at the academic record. Exceptionally high
scores coupled with low grades may signal the admissions
director that he is dealing with a student who hasn't
applied himself very seriously and might continue this
pattern in college. So don't count on acing the SAT as a
way to make up for four years of goofing off in high school.
"We will always take a student with strong school performance and weak scores over someone with weak performance and strong scores," says Steven Syverson of
Lawrence University, who has lots of company.

Though it obviously helps to have high scores, the critical thing is to fall in the college's general range. Don't be
too concerned with mean or median scores. (See Chapter
9, "Lies, Damned Lies and Statistics.") You're in good
shape if you're between the 25th and 75th percentile of
their SAT profile.

THE BOTTOM LINE

It is clear that the SAT and other tests still hold consid-
erable sway in most college admissions offices. According
to Robert Fraley of Pepperdine University, "In a time
when practically everyone judges a college by its freshman profile, an admissions committee would be foolish to
deny 1200 SATs and take 800 SATs."

Many admissions officers have doubts about the SAT,

but they cannot bring themselves to discount it because they fear their academic profile might not look as good. All too many colleges publicly downplay their use of the SAT in admissions even though the test continues to be an important factor in most decisions.

What it all boils down to: Don't take standardized tests too seriously or too lightly. Like any other important test, you should do your best, but realize that it isn't the end of the world if the kid down the street gets a better score. Your worth as a human being—or as a potential freshman—cannot be reduced to a three-digit number. After all, when was the last time you saw a tombstone with SAT scores inscribed on it?

13

TO CRAM OR NOT TO CRAM?

You've seen the ads. They all say something like "Super Duper Test Prep: Increase Your SAT Score 150 Points—Guaranteed!!" And then the fine print: "Only $500 for four sessions."

By now you must be wondering whether all these high-priced test prep outfits are really as good as they're cracked up to be. Unfortunately, there's no definitive answer to that question. Some people's scores go up drastically after taking a prep course; other people's actually go down, and still others' stay about the same. "You pay your money and you take your chances," says Ronald Potier of Franklin and Marshall College.

So what did you expect? Two 800s on a silver platter?

While the value of short-term cram courses is debatable, there are some things about preparing for the SAT that we can say for sure.

GET A HEAD START

Everybody agrees that the BEST way to prepare is to work hard in school. On the verbal part, lots of reading and good conversation with intelligent people (maybe even your parents) is the best recipe for success. If you're really on the ball, you could begin studying vocabulary lists about six months before the test and probably hike your verbal score fifty points.

For the math part, doing well in school is also key, and you should definitely brush up on the types of equations you're most likely to see on the test. There is little doubt that a long-term study plan for the SAT will pay off. If your school offers such a program, look into it.

Since they are more closely tied to school curriculums, you can definitely improve your scores on the ACT or Achievement Tests by studying for them. Here, too, a long-term approach is best, but as much last-minute cramming as you can do should also be helpful.

BIG BUCKS AND BIGGER PROMISES

Theoretically, the short-term approach won't do much good for the SAT since it covers too much information to learn in a short period of time. (At least that is the official line of the Educational Testing Service, which prepares and administers the test.)

In recent years, numerous "quick fix" coaching operations run by private, profit-making companies have sprung up across the nation. These groups claim to be able to raise scores in the span of a few weeks—not by expanding your vocabulary or reading comprehension, but by teaching you HOW to take the test. Often, the emphasis is less on real learning than on figuring out what the test maker had in mind when he made up the question so you can "beat him at his own game." In exchange for their advice, these coaching outfits typically charge hundreds of dollars.

ADMISSIONS OFFICERS KEEP MUM

Do these short-term cram courses really work?

Many admissions directors think they do but are reluctant to say so. According to one who asked not to be identified, "I promote professionally the ETS stand that coaching is limited in its results—then I go off the record and say it depends on the student."

Prime candidates for a prep course include students who have gone to mediocre high schools—and would benefit from some extra drilling—or students who merely want to build confidence as they approach test day.

Or if you're one of those people who simply don't test well, an SAT prep course might be a good time for some intensive work on your test-taking skills.

In addition, since many people believe that prep courses are most effective for the math section, students applying to technical schools would do well to consider a course.

GET WHAT YOU PAY FOR

Before you sign up at a particular agency, find out exactly what you'll be learning.

Is the primary emphasis on vocabulary words and equations? Or merely "psyching out the test"? And how long is the course? In general, the longer it is, the more likely it will make a difference.

If you are thinking seriously of taking a coaching course, try to do it before the first time you take the test, which will probably be in the spring of your junior year. What you want to avoid is an upward blip in your score between the first and second time you take the test. Each time you take a standardized test, all your previous scores are reported again. If you happen to improve a great deal the second time after being coached, this could raise suspicion that your score is artificially high—the result of a cram course. On pain of death, don't announce (as some do) that you're taking one. Admissions people don't want to know.

If you do take the test without prepping and are disappointed, you might still consider a course, but only if you think you can improve substantially. On the other hand, if you do well on the SAT the first time—say, the 50th percentile or above at the schools you're interested in—consign your College Board pamphlets to the attic and move on to other things. (See Chapter 12, "How Important Is the SAT?")

THE TRIED-AND-TRUE METHOD

The alternative to taking a course is to prepare on your own. In addition to the long-term plan outlined above, you should buy one or more prep books, which are on sale at any bookstore. (See Chapter 6, "Recommended Reading.") These typically include vocabulary lists, mathematical equations and some practice tests published by the College Board. The main thing is to familiarize yourself with the test format so you won't have to spend time reading directions when you take the test for real.

SOME SEE A SCANDAL

The current vogue of SAT prep courses has become an embarrassment to many in admissions.

"The SAT craze has become a scandal, and I believe the traffic in 'prep' courses is *prima facie* evidence of that fact," says Douglas Paschall of the University of the South. A few admissions directors, notably Richard Skelton of Bucknell and Cal Black of Wabash, report that they are relying on the SAT less than they used to.

But for the moment, the SAT is here to stay. And so too, it seems, are SAT prep courses. Ideally, every high school student should curl up with a copy of *Moby Dick* and a good dictionary. But until that day comes, prep courses will be a viable alternative. They cost a pretty penny, but if you think that you can improve your scores by taking one, there is no reason why you shouldn't consider it.

14

HOW TO SIZE UP A CAMPUS

Visiting campuses should be the most exciting stage of the college search. After months of hearing secondhand reports, this is your chance to see real college students in their native habitat and get a taste of the lifestyle that awaits you after high school. Whether or not you make a wise decision could hinge on how observant you are, so come prepared to make the most of it.

Plan Ahead. The first step is to make plans early. It's best to schedule your visit when classes are in session, but a visit in the summer is better than no visit at all. Since interview schedules at popular schools fill up fast, you should try to call several months ahead of time to make an appointment. (A note to the faint of heart: It's your visit so YOU make the call, not your parents.)

If you're planning to stay overnight—which you should do if at all possible—ask the admissions office if you can sleep in the dorms. If you want to arrange meetings with professors, coaches, etc., or if there are particular programs that you'd like to learn about in depth, now is the time to make the arrangements.

If It's Friday, This Must Be . . . Friday is generally the best day of the week to visit, since you can sample both weekday and weekend activity.

Though it is natural to want to fit in as many colleges as possible, it is best not to see more than one—and at the most two—in a day. Trying to cram too many in, says William Hiss of Bates College, usually results in a student "screaming at Mother or Father to hurry up and find the college when they are lost and five minutes late for the interview."

On the other hand, if you live near a college you are considering, you may have the luxury of visiting more than once. If you do, our advice is to go once with your parents to get the standard information from the admissions office, and once on your own to stay in the dorms and sample student life.

Sizing Yourself Up Redux. As the visit approaches, do some hard thinking about what is most important to you in a college.

Is the quality of the history department really that big a deal to you? Are you dead set on going to a school with a strong Greek system? Do dance facilities still loom as large in your mind as they did six months ago?

Once you've settled on some criteria, make a list of the questions you want answered and establish a uniform way of recording your impressions so you can compare different schools on key points.

Cutting Through the Baloney. On the appointed day try to get there early, especially if you have any appointments. (See Chapter 16, "Surviving the Interview.") Once you've gotten those out of the way, take a campus tour. It will probably be led by a student—though by no means a typical one. The grinning, affable, oh-so-polite "representatives" that most colleges choose as tour guides can lay it on pretty thick.

See if your tour guide will admit to anything negative

about his or her school; that should give you a good idea of how much of the positive stuff you can believe. Whether your guide is completely candid or not, the tour is valuable because it offers one student's perspective on the college, which you can compare to that of your interviewer and anyone else you happen to meet.

Don't Be Shy. While the interview is the place to get the ins and outs of particular programs, the tour is usually best for information about student life.

Though most high school students seem to develop a sudden case of laryngitis during a campus tour, that doesn't mean you have to be mute, too. For goodness' sake, ask a question! What are the dorms like? Where do people go to have fun? What are the biggest issues on campus?

Don't be afraid to dig beyond the stock answers. "Colleges often boast about their facilities," says Olga Euben of Hampshire College, "but who gets to use them? Can a student who isn't a computer major use the computers?" Likewise, if the guide says the library is big, find out if it is open-stack. Do freshmen have the same privileges as seniors or graduate students?

There are dozens of questions you could ask, but see the box below for five we think are especially penetrating.

Five Good Questions to Ask Your Tour Guide

- *Who will teach me?* Do senior faculty teach the general-education courses that all students must take during their freshman and sophomore years? If they don't, you should wonder whether the institution takes undergraduate education seriously.

- *How big are freshman classes?* Forget about student–faculty ratios. Find out how big your classes will be during your first year.
- *What happens on a typical weekend?* This will give you a sense of the overall character of the student body, as well as the range of options that would be open to you as a student.
- *Do students talk about current issues?* Casual conversation says a lot about the intellectual atmosphere of a college. Political and social issues play a key role in student life at some and are hardly ever mentioned at others. Find out if students would rather talk about South Africa or Saturday night.
- *What are this college's biggest weaknesses?* The answer should be revealing.

Keep Your Eyes Peeled. In addition to being a good question-and-answer session, the tour will give you a sense for the layout of the campus.

Keep an eye out for bulletin boards; they will give you a good idea of what is going on that week. Note the condition of the buildings. Facilities in disrepair are a sign of a college with financial problems, while new construction is a sign of health. Be sure to ask the guide about any facilities you expected to see if they are not on the route. At the very least, the guide can point them out to you on a campus map.

Poke Around On Your Own. Don't just settle for the standard public relations tour. Leave time to roam the campus on your own.

This is no time for bashfulness: Corner some students and see if their answers jibe with those you got from the tour guide. "Honesty will prevail . . . whether we in admissions like it or not," says Martha Quirk of Principia College.

Obvious places to roam include libraries, classrooms, the dorms and the student center or other central gathering place. See if you can feel the pulse of the campus. Do the students seem friendly? Intellectual? Jocky? Are they radical chic? Or does it feel like you've just stumbled onto the set of *Revenge of the Nerds*?

"You've got to ask, 'Are these my kind of people?' " says Glenn Sklarin of Brooklyn College. Sit in on a class, eat a meal in the dining hall, go to a sports event. What's your gut reaction? According to Ann Quinley of the University of Connecticut, "It is not so much a matter of what you see but rather how you feel about the campus. It is rather like trying on a suit or a dress or driving a car; some just 'fit' better than others."

Things to Notice on Campus

- *Buildings in disrepair*—the signal of a college with financial problems. One good place to check out: the bathrooms.
- *New construction*—a sign of financial health and a statement of the college's priorities.

- *Seating in the cafeteria*—Are students sitting at the same tables with faculty members? Blacks with whites? A good indication of social relationships on campus.
- *Library stacks*—Does the library have open stacks that allow everyone to browse, or do you have to order books from the librarian? A statement about how high a priority the typical student is.
- *Size of classrooms*—Lots of lecture halls suggest big classes. Lots of seminar rooms mean a more personalized approach.
- *Bulletin boards*—the single best authority on what students care about.
- *The campus store*—What it stocks is a good sign of what students value. If it has more sweatshirts than quality paperbacks, then caveat emptor.

Sample the Nightlife. If you're staying in the dorms, your host or hostess will be a gold mine of information. Get him or her to show you around and see how it compares to your official tour. If you're interested in a particular program, ask if he or she has any friends who are enrolled in it, and give them a call.

In the evening, relax and hang out with whoever happens to be in the dorm. Apply what Philip Smith of Williams College calls "the 10:30 test." Says he: "Almost all college students get hungry around 10:30 P.M. Between then and midnight tends to be 'people time.' Find out what students are talking about, how they treat one another, the depth of their concerns." Try to stay up for as much of it as you can. Sometimes the most interesting conversations don't really get started until two or three in the morning.

What Did You Think? As the visit draws to a close, be sure to get your thoughts down on paper while they're still fresh in your mind. Note all the particulars about the academic programs and facilities, but also remember the big picture. Above all, trust your instincts about the people and the place. Could you see yourself as a student there? Four years is a long time.

15

THE BEST
COLLEGE TOWNS

They say that if you're ever in a Cambridge supermarket and the guy in front of you in the express checkout line has fifteen items instead of the allotted ten, he's either an MIT student who can't read or a Harvard student who can't count. And so it goes in Cambridge.

College towns come with their own little idiosyncrasies. The colleges that reside in and around the towns contribute to this flavor and flair, just as the characteristics of the town can't help but rub off on the college and its students.

Remember when you're making your college visits not to take the town for granted. Investigate the campus's immediate neighborhood as well as its proximity to a bustling city or a peaceful mountain setting. Depending upon where your recreational or preprofessional interests lie, these factors can make a big difference.

Here are quickie portraits of eight of the best college towns in the country. You can see how different personalities might be drawn to each one.

AUSTIN, Texas, is a bustling state capital with rapidly expanding business and government industries that provide excellent internship and co-op opportunities . . . home of the sprawling flagship school of the University of Texas system and a few small Christian colleges . . . situated deep in the heart of Texas, but not too far for weekend road trips to Houston or Dallas . . . downtown is Sixth Street, a six-block strip with more than seventy clubs, restaurants and theaters . . . adjacent to the university's main campus is "the Drag," a popular retail and gathering strip for students . . . chicken-fried steak, hearty Tex-Mex cooking and plenty of fiestas year-round . . . Symphony Square is an outdoor amphitheater, its stage and seating area bisected by Waller Creek . . . every kind of music from progressive country to uptown jazz . . . the finest stretch of lake country in the Texas hills starts in Austin with an oasis of fishing and boating, swimming and scuba-diving lakes . . . an abundance of bike trails surrounds the lakes . . . Ziller Park, Austin's largest and most beautiful city park, hosts a Fall Jazz Festival . . . Barton Springs pool, Austin's spring-fed natural swimming pool, is nearly as long as a football field and is always 68 degrees . . . ahhhh.

BATON ROUGE, Louisiana, is the home of Louisiana State University, extremely rowdy Tiger football games and arguably the best tailgate parties in the country . . . the capital of a state that holds over fifty festivals a year . . . only seventy-seven miles from New Orleans, where Tulane University, Xavier University and the University of New Orleans all reside . . . February means Mardi Gras and everyone gets two days off from school to go . . . every April, LSU hosts the Jambalaya Jamboree (better known as Jam Jam), complete with games and a dance contest . . . plenty of down-home Cajun and Creole cooking—jambalaya and crawfish . . . sweet southern hospitality . . . loads of camping and hiking opportunities in nearby parks and wildlife preserves . . . only an hour's drive to the French Louisiana country of the bayous, with marshes and lakes for boating, water skiing and fishing . . . mild, almost semitropical climate year-round . . . downtown, along the banks of the Mississippi River, there's Catfish Town, a marketplace with festive shops and restaurants . . . y'all come down now, ya hear?

BLOOMINGTON, Indiana, belongs to Indiana University and the main campus of the state system belongs to Bloomington . . . almost 33,000 students in a town of 53,000 . . . but Purdue University is only two hours away and Indiana State University is about an hour . . . basketball reigns supreme . . . every April brings IU's "Little 500," a bicycle race and party that has been called one of the world's greatest college weekends . . . more than 1,000 musical events a year . . . Brown County State Park, just east of Bloomington, provides opportunities for hiking, camping and horseback riding . . . old limestone quarries have caves for spelunking and water basins for scuba diving and swimming . . . Nashville, Indiana, just about twenty minutes down the road, offers everything from skiing to home-made apple butter plus crafts, hand-made furniture, jewelry, and leaf tours . . . about eight miles south is Lake Monroe for sailing catamarans, boating, swimming, lots of water skiing, para skiing . . . every fall there's HoosierFest, a four-day fall event complete with balloon races, live bands, a barbecue cook-off and a pig roast . . . because the main industry here is student pleasing, downtown is filled with cheap eateries that specialize in fried biscuits, deep-dish pizza and stromboli sandwiches, a.k.a. "stroms" . . . housing is cheap, cheap, cheap.

BOSTON and **CAMBRIDGE, Massachusetts,** combined create what is universally known as the quintessential college town . . . with more colleges—Harvard, MIT, Boston University, Tufts, Boston College, to name a few— per square foot than any other city in the country . . . internship and co-op possibilities abound in this politically active state capital . . . fantastic seafood and baked beans . . . Faneuil Hall marketplace and Newbury Street with their great watering holes, restaurants and shops . . . home of Steve's Ice Cream . . . Harvard Square for just hanging out . . . Inman Square for excellent jazz . . . the Celtics for basketball fanatics . . . the Charles River for rowing, sailing or riding bikes and running along the banks . . . the Head of the Charles annual regatta for meeting students from all over New England . . . only about an hour from Cape Cod . . . less than two hours from great skiing in Vermont and New Hampshire . . . outdoor concerts on the Boston Common and the Hatch Shell down by the river.

BURLINGTON, Vermont, is "The Queen City" of the state . . . situated along the eastern shore of the 120-mile Lake Champlain, which makes for lots of swimming, sailing, wind surfing, powerboating and fishing when it's warm, not to mention great ice skating when it's nippy . . . the University of Vermont, Champlain College, Trinity College and Burlington College are all in this area . . . the only city in the country with a socialist mayor . . . hopping downtown nightlife along the waterfront . . . the Church Street Marketplace, a four-block pedestrian mall with more than a hundred bars, shops and restaurants lining the waterfront . . . lots of maple syrup and cheese . . . the Annual Champlain Valley Fair and the Vermont State Fair every fall . . . camping, hunting, hiking, backpacking, horseback riding, golfing and even stock car racing nearby . . . 45 minutes from skiing at Stowe . . . surrounded by the Green Mountains to the east and facing the Adirondacks across the lake . . . unbeatable fall foliage.

CHAPEL HILL, North Carolina, a.k.a. "The Southern Part of Heaven" . . . has the look and feel of a remote southern village with only 33,000 people . . . home of the University of North Carolina and only twenty-eight miles away from North Carolina State in Raleigh, the state capital . . . Durham and Duke University are only a bike ride away . . . Franklin Street is packed with college students, movie theaters and eateries that offer everything from Greek fast food on a pita to Italian ice cream

in a waffle cone . . . a few hours to the west are mountains
for skiing, hiking or camping . . . a few hours to the east
lie miles of eastern seashore . . . together Chapel Hill,
Raleigh and Durham make up the famous Research Tri-
angle, which provides undergraduate internship and co-
op opportunities with government, private industry and
educational organizations . . . mild weather year-round
. . . plenty of affordable housing.

EUGENE, Oregon, is an outdoorsy person's paradise
. . . known as the running capital of the world with its
miles of running and bicycle paths, including Pre's Trail,
a specially designed European-style jogging and exercise
course . . . the University of Oregon shares Eugene with
Northwestern Christian College and Eugene Bible College . . . there are numerous golf courses and emerald
green rivers for canoeing and rafting . . . snow-capped
mountains to the east . . . nearby is some of the finest
downhill skiing in the country . . . cross-country ski trails
can be found ten minutes from Eugene . . . just an hour
to the west are the sand dunes and beaches of the Oregon

coast . . . hundreds of crystal-clear lakes . . . miles of wilderness for campers and backpackers to roam, including the Pacific Crest Hiking Trail . . . the Fern Ridge Reservoir, a popular sailing and swimming site . . . 1,600 acres of city park land . . . Hendricks Park, where more than 6,000 rhododendrons and azaleas grow . . . the temperature is moderate year-round; the winter temp rarely dips below freezing . . . annual Eugene Empire Rodeo . . . the downtown Valley River Center has restaurants, cinemas, cabarets and nightclubs.

TEMPE, Arizona, is known as "The Valley of the Sun" . . . home of Arizona State University and part of the Phoenix metropolitan area but separated from the hustle and bustle of the city . . . lots of blue skies, wide-open space and easy living . . . ASU's Gammage Center for the Performing Arts, a landmark hall, designed by Frank Lloyd Wright, provides nonstop entertainment—musicals and dance performances, jazz and big-band concerts, narrated films . . . bike paths and fitness trails are plentiful . . . Sun Devil Village, a mass of inexpensive apartments, bars, restaurants and cinemas . . . a man-made beach complete with a wave machine is nearby . . . in every direction, there are mountains for climbing and ranges for hiking, backpacking and horseback riding.

16

SURVIVING
THE INTERVIEW

It is a scene every college applicant comes to dread: the awkward quiet of an admissions office waiting room, filled with nervous students and parents awaiting the call from within. Mother leans over to straighten your collar as you stare blankly at the pages of a catalog. The wait seems like an eternity, but finally an admissions officer beckons and ushers you into her office. After a brief exchange of pleasantries, she asks what books you have read lately.

"None!" you blurt out suddenly. "I hate reading!" With that, you leap to your feet, lift your chair high in the air and smash it to splinters on top of her desk. As she flees the room in terror, you watch her with a fiendish gleam in your eye, and laugh and laugh and laugh . . .

Fortunately for those with active imaginations, few applicants actually go berserk in the interview. What's more, the interview isn't nearly as important in the admissions process as most people seem to think.

At many schools, such as Colgate and St. John's College, the interview is nothing more than an information session for the benefit of the applicant. Even colleges that use them for admissions purposes realize that twenty minutes of chit-chat may not reveal much about the real you—especially if you're nervous. When it does count, the interview almost always works in the student's favor. As James Holmes of Washington College notes, "It's rare that someone shoots himself in the foot with some horrendous blunder."

Before you hit the panic button about the interview, check with the admissions office to find out what their policy is. Are the interviews strictly informational, or are they used in making decisions? Remember, too, that the interview isn't so much a judgment of you as it is one more step in the college matchmaking process. "We have no hidden agenda," says Natalie Aharonian of Wellesley College. "It is a genuine opportunity for her to tell us what she considers significant about herself. It is also a chance for her to learn more about us."

If a college interview is like a first date with a potential mate, it makes sense to want to put your best foot forward. Here are a few tips:

TRY TO RELAX

The interviewer knows you are going to be nervous, and he or she will almost never hold it against you. After all, it shows you care. Ninety-nine times out of a hundred, the admissions officer will do his or her best to put you at ease.

If—God forbid—something does happen, have a sense of humor. This worked for at least one stressed-out applicant to Franklin and Marshall College, who, sitting with her legs crossed, was so nervous that she kept swinging her foot back and forth. It just so happened that she was wearing clogs. On a particularly long swing, the clog flew off, hit the admissions officer in the head and then ricocheted off his desk lamp, breaking it. "She looked at him in terror," says Ronald Potier of F&M, "but when their glances met, they both dissolved in laughter." No big deal.

BE PREPARED

You yourself should make all the arrangements for the interview and see to it that you arrive at least fifteen minutes early to check in.

Do your homework on the school ahead of time and come armed with at least three questions. Good questions, mind you. While an admissions officers is likely to be impressed by a probing question, he is just as likely to be turned off by a stupid one ("Do you have a psychology major?") that is answered on the first page of the viewbook. (See Chapter 17, "No-No's.") By asking intelligent questions, you let the admissions officer know that you are going about the matchmaking process carefully. That in itself is a big point in your favor.

Some Good Questions to Ask Your Interviewer

- *What is distinctive about your school?* Try to get beyond the usual platitudes about academic excellence. Each school has a different idea of its mission, which tells you a lot about its character.
- *What sets students here apart from those at similar schools?* If this is Yale, ask about the differences from Harvard or Princeton. You'll probably be considering those competing schools, too, so try to zero in on where each one stands in relation to the others.
- *What is the retention rate?* What percentage of entering students return for their sophomore year and graduate within five years? If the rate is low, find out why.
- *What are your most recent alumni doing?* Is the school a feeder for Wall Street, or does everybody join the Peace Corps after graduation? Find out

whether the aspirations of past graduates match yours.
- *Would I have been accepted last year?* Whether or not you get into a selective college depends mainly on who you're competing against. Since admissions officers can't predict the exact mix of applicants in any given year, asking about last year makes it easier for them to assess your chances.

EXPECT TOUGH QUESTIONS

Interviewers will rarely try to embarrass you, but there are certain time-honored zingers that you ought to be ready for.
- *What books have you read lately?* If the last one was *Cat in the Hat,* perhaps it's time you visited the library. The purpose of the question is to test both your curiosity and your analytical skills. If possible, pick a book that really excites you and that you wouldn't mind discussing at length. An in-depth talk about a book you know well will almost always impress an interviewer. By the same token, if you try to wing it, you'll look like a liar and an idiot at the same time.

Ten Books You Should Definitely Not Cite as Your Favorites

Babar Goes to the Country
Call of the Wild
Charlotte's Web
The Closing of the American Mind
Gone With the Wind

Green Eggs and Ham
How to Ace the SAT
Lord of the Flies
Rin-Tin-Tin
The Scarlet Letter
The Wizard of Oz

• *Why do you want to come here?* The trick is to cite at least two or three reasons. Read the college's literature and mention what you've found there—diversity, academic excellence, etc.—and mix that with some reasons of your own, like the fact that it is strong in the natural sciences or has good performing arts facilities. Strike a balance between the things you are interested in and the things the college is trying to sell you on.

• *What are your most important activities and why are they valuable?* Think this out before the interview, and resist the temptation to be too grandiose. Standard answers that cite benefits such as increased self-discipline and experience working with others are fine. If you can think of something more extraordinary—such as an experience that has been a turning point in your life—so much the better.

• *What would you add to life at this college?* Let's face it, Prestige U. isn't waiting for you on pins and needles. Not to worry. Just list some ways that you would affect the lives of others in the community. The purpose of the question is to find out how much you would give of yourself to those around you. Colleges want givers.

• *What other colleges are you considering?* This one is loaded. On the one hand, your list will tell the college something about you and your interests. Your interviewer will know all about all the other schools and will be impressed if you can explain your choices cogently. If the list includes colleges that are radically different from one another, explain. Otherwise, it will appear that you haven't done a very good job of researching.

On the other hand, the list will give the interviewer an idea of whether his or her college is your first choice—something uppermost in the minds of admissions officers at schools that are usually safeties. If the college is your first choice, stress that fact. If it's your safety, be a little vague. It is always best to give the impression that the college is among your top choices.

BE YOURSELF

Again, the interview is a time for an honest exchange between you and the college to see if there is a good match. A put-on job defeats the whole purpose of match-making. (See Chapter 17, "No-No's.") Nothing will impress the interviewer more than spontaneity, genuineness and sincere interest. Says Jennifer Trussell of Mississippi College, "Nobody likes a know-it-all student. A sense of openness, honesty and humor is a real plus."

BE UPBEAT—AND LEAVE YOUR SNAKES AT HOME

Admissions officers much prefer people who are upbeat and enthusiastic to those who are cynical. Try to highlight what sets you apart from other applicants, and be prepared to talk at length about a favorite subject or activity. If you have some impressive examples of your work in hobbies or extracurricular activities, consider bringing one to show your interviewer.

We don't, however, recommend the example related by Larry Mench of Dickinson College, who recalls one applicant who actually uncoiled a fifteen-foot boa constrictor on his desk. According to Mench, "The young man was admitted with a special request that he leave his snakes at home."

DON'T BRING MOM AND DAD

If this really were your first date with a potential mate, would you want your parents along? Mom and Dad mean well, but the interview is about you and you only.

Let your parents take a tour of the campus and meet you after you're finished. There is absolutely nothing a parent can do to help in the interview, but every admissions officer has horror stories of overanxious parents spoiling it for their son or daughter. Says Lorna Blake of Smith, "Your parents are more nervous than you are, so don't let them take over in the reception room." (Yet again—see Chapter 17, "No-No's.")

It is, of course, legitimate for parents to ask questions of the admissions officer, but only after the interview is over, and then only if they have a chance to do so without appearing pushy or overprotective.

17

NO-NO'S:
FIVE SURE WAYS TO
BLOW YOUR CHANCES

Just for a moment, see if you can put yourself inside an admissions officer's shoes. Imagine yourself having to deal with all those stressed-out students and parents parading in YOUR office day after day. Some of them would do anything. "I have been threatened, cursed and hugged," says John Beacon of the University of Nebraska. "The most interesting one was when I was solicited by the mother of a student." He didn't accept.

Fortunately, most admissions officers are kindhearted souls who like working with young people and are slow to anger. But they have their limits. As part of our survey, we asked them to list some of the things that really get under their skin. Here are the five biggest ones:

1. PUSHY PARENTS

If there is one thing that peeves admissions officers more than anything else, it is parents who take control of the admissions process and won't let their children speak for themselves. Charles Wharton of Austin College remembers one overeager mother who monopolized the interview bragging about her daughter's voice. "I wouldn't know," he finally replied. "I haven't heard it yet."

At Le Moyne College, one father of a pre-med hopeful wrapped up the interview by telling his son to get up and walk around the room. The father then proudly proclaimed, "Look, look—he even walks like a doctor." In an interview with the parents of an applicant to the University of Michigan, admissions director Cliff Sjogren was presented with an expensive and impressive portfolio of their work (they both were architects) and the admonition that "if I did not admit their daughter, I would miss out on a student who had a highly desirable genetic background." Their daughter was rejected because of low grades and test scores.

2. PASSIVE APPLICANTS

The flip side of the pushy-parent syndrome, this is when students are content to let their parents and guidance counselor do all the work of applying for them. This type of student generally uses what Don Lautenbach of Calvin College calls "a prehistoric vocabulary"—"uh-huh, uh-huh and mmmm"—in the interview and cannot be goaded into a conversation of any kind. He or she generally does whatever Mom and Dad say.

3. UNINFORMED APPLICANTS

This is the kind of applicant who will travel thousands of miles for an interview only to find that the college doesn't offer the program he wants. Admissions officers tell of students who don't bother to read their literature—and then ask obvious questions in the interview—as one of the things they hate most. Equally nettlesome, however, are applicants who don't have any questions at all.

The upshot? Know enough about the college to ask *intelligent* questions.

4. IMAGE MONGERS

Time and again, admissions officers cite overly "prepped" applicants as one of their biggest annoyances. "We tire of applicants who try too hard to beat the system by 'packaging' themselves," says Linda Davis of Amherst College. Particularly irritating are those who play the "junior exec" role to follow in Daddy's footsteps. Such applicants usually come to the interview with a prerehearsed spiel and are unwilling to engage in the give-and-take of a real conversation.

5. BULLIES

This is a big one.

Admissions officers absolutely hate to be bullied by thinly veiled threats of outside influence. Any kind of bragging about important friends, background, wealth, etc., is the kiss of death.

Sally Austin of Goucher College abhorred the comment of one father of a prospective student who wanted to know "how much my son will make after graduation if he attends your college."

One father demanded a second interview after his son had been rejected from Ursinus College. His opening line in this important conversation was to tell the admissions counselor, "I bet you wish you earned in a year what I get back on my tax return."

Outright bribe attempts, such as one applicant's offer of $10,000 for admission to George Mills of the University of Puget Sound, are guaranteed to fail. Likewise, recommendations from big-shot friends of the family are always worthless. (See Chapter 19, "Getting Good Recommendations.") Ninety-nine times out of a hundred, if the applicant can't get in on his or her own, he or she won't get in at all.

18

THE RIGHT WAY TO FILL OUT AN APPLICATION

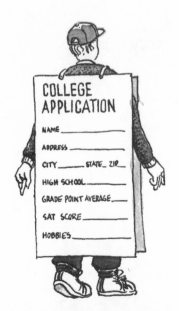

Sometimes college applicants defy all logic. They're willing to foot a hefty bill for SAT preparation and outside counseling, fork over hundreds on application fees, and travel across the country to visit colleges. But when it comes time to fill out their applications, they dash them off in an hour or two without even bothering to proofread.

That, say the admissions directors we surveyed, is a fatal mistake.

Keep in mind, the application is *you* in the eyes of the admissions office. As Martha Quirk of Principia College in Illinois puts it, "It usually represents a lot of who that person is, his values, his insights and his strengths and weaknesses."

With so much riding on the application, it pays to handle it with the utmost care. Here are a few tidbits of advice:

BE NEAT

The moment you get a college's application in your hot little hands, make at least two photocopies. Don't mark on the original until you've gotten all the typos, misspellings, and tomato-sauce stains out of your system. Also, read the directions carefully before you begin to make sure you won't have to go back and change something.

A neat application, according to Ann Wright of the University of Rochester, is like having a clean house: "You don't always get credit for it, but if it's cluttered or dirty, the effect is disastrous."

GET IT IN EARLY

You'll save yourself a panic at deadline time, and maybe even boost your admissions chances to boot. Tim Rinehart of the University of Massachusetts at Amherst warns that applications "submitted in the last week tend to get caught in the last big wave and may get less attention."

FILL IT OUT YOURSELF

If Mommy and Daddy's fingerprints show up on the application anywhere—for example, if it has two different kinds of handwriting—you've got a credibility problem. Get them to proofread it if you like, but write or type it yourself. It doesn't have to be immaculate, just legible.

"We're not looking for perfect people—human ones," says Linda Davis of Amherst College. "Let your personality shine through."

USE YOUR HEAD

When the application asks for a Visa number, don't fill in the one from Dad's credit card. The question is meant for foreigners, a fact that will be clear if you read the application carefully. Likewise, don't answer with strained attempts at humor. One admissions director cited with disgust the applicant who listed one of his favorite activities as "beating my grandmother with a tire iron." Ugh! The short-answer questions are not the time to be funny.

Be a Copycat

Always make a photocopy of any application materials that pass through your hands. That goes for recommendation forms, the transcript, the application—everything. If you're lucky, no one will misplace anything you give them and nothing will get lost in the mail.

If you're lucky.

DON'T LIST TOO MANY ACTIVITIES

A laundry list takes credibility away from the ones that are really important to you. It is far better to mention two or three that you were genuinely committed to than the ten that you dabbled in. Make sure you list the most important ones first, and if possible, elaborate on their significance to you in the essay or interview.

EXPLAIN EVERYTHING

If you were chairperson of the Founder's Day Committee, it won't mean anything to the admissions office unless you explain what you did and why the committee was important. Likewise, if there's a black mark on your transcript—like a suspension or a bad grade—don't just hope that the admissions office won't notice. If there's any explanation you can give without sounding whiny or bitter, attach a note on a separate sheet.

Some students may be tempted to send along some extra material to supplement the application, like tapes of a musical performance or a portfolio of art work. Extra exhibits can be useful, but only if they help round out your profile in the eyes of the admissions office with new information not already in the application (see Chapter 24, "Gimmicks").

In the words of William Hiss of Bates College in Maine, "I don't need a chocolate layer cake, your kindergarten report card, or all the poems you wrote in the ninth grade. I am very interested in seeing the results of whatever it was you consider your finest accomplishment, whether that be photographs of your set designs, or genetics research, or Scottish dancing."

19

GETTING GOOD RECOMMENDATIONS

There is a rule of thumb among admissions officers that "the thicker the file, the thicker the kid."

What that means, in practical terms, is that if you're thinking of padding up your application with a gaggle of letters of recommendation from well-placed friends of the family, forget it. "Each year we run an informal contest to determine the candidate with the largest number of superfluous recommendations," reports Robert Jones of Hampden-Sydney College. "This year's winner had twenty-three, and he was denied."

Don't misunderstand. Recommendations can be useful, but *only* from people who know you well. A good one will tell the admissions committee something about you personally that comes out nowhere else on the application— your willingness to work hard, perhaps, or your ability to listen to good advice and then use it. Recommendations that begin with phrases like "I don't know Susie personally, but if she is anything like her parents . . ." are a cinch to start eyes glazing.

ACCENT ON ACADEMICS

To get good recommendations, find people who know you well, are familiar with your goals and aspirations, and can write about you in concrete detail. (You won't be able to look at the recommendations before they're sent, so choose carefully.) Most colleges require at least two recommendations from teachers. Since colleges want to know "what you've done for me lately," try to pick teachers who have taught you in your junior or senior year.

English teachers tend to write well, so they are usually a good bet. Those in other core subjects like math or social studies may also fit the bill, but try to avoid coaches or teachers of fluffy electives. Even if you are pals with the yearbook sponsor, your math teacher is likely to have more clout with the admissions office.

In general, it is best to pick a teacher who respects you as a person and who can testify to some of your deeper and less obvious qualities. Says Tim Fuller from Houghton College, "If a student has cruised through a class and gotten an A, a recommendation from that teacher concerning his or her natural abilities may not be as helpful to the student's admission chances as one where the student has had to struggle and work hard to get a B."

Your Rights Under the Buckley Amendment

You might not know it, but because of an act of Congress you have the right to look at your recommendations *after* they are filed at the colleges. The issue is complex, dealing with limits to your right to privacy, but the upshot is this: Most recommendation forms have a place to check off if you want to sign away your rights under the Buckley Amendment. We think you should. If you waive your right to see your recommendation, your recommender will feel freer to be candid, and the college will be reassured that you are not worried about what your recommender might say.

GUIDANCE: HANDLE WITH CARE

Many colleges require a recommendation from the guidance office. How useful this recommendation is likely to be will hinge on how much firsthand information the counselor has about you.

At a small high school, the counselor often knows everyone and can provide a good overview of your academic career based on his or her knowledge and input from a number of teachers. At larger ones, there's little chance of that happening unless you're an academic superstar. The only way the counselor will know firsthand of your work is if you yourself keep him or her up to date.

In either case, it is a good idea to establish a personal relationship with the counselor to avoid a recommendation confined to meaningless generalities. (See Chapter 5, "Getting Help.") Otherwise, you run the risk of suffering a fate similar to the luckless applicant to St. John's College in New Mexico who had a recommendation that said simply, "Joe is really amazing. He does things that are just not normal."

DON'T DILLY-DALLY

Having chosen your recommender, don't be bashful. Responsible teachers will rarely say no, but if they hint that someone else might be better, by all means heed their advice.

Popular teachers tend to be snowed under with requests by December, so try to get to them early and make the process as painless as possible for them.

Make It Easy

Along with the form, be sure to give your recommender an addressed, stamped envelope that can be mailed to the admissions office. It may help as well to prepare a brief synopsis of your goals and accomplishments so that the recommender can write knowledgeably about you.

If you happen to choose a teacher who seems uncertain about what to write, advise him or her to be candid, specific and to the point, using as few vague generalities as possible. Encourage him or her to quote specific anecdotes, such as the times you stayed after school to get help, or how you did four drafts of a term paper to get it right.

HOW THICK IS TOO THICK?

Occasionally, it may be appropriate to send along an extra character recommendation beyond those asked for on the application. But mind you, do it only if another person can say something important about your candidacy beyond what is already in the application. There is a right—and wrong—way to go about it.

Consider the examples brought to us by William J. Buchanan of Virginia Military Institute: "We had an alumnus solicit letters of recommendation for his son from his 200+ VMI classmates; no dice. . . . One applicant (over 1400 SAT) sent letters of recommendation from an archbishop, an illiterate scoutmaster, and a man signing himself as a former captain in the Czar's Imperial Guard; no sale again (this lad got As in courses he liked and Fs in those he didn't)." The reason these examples were no good? No personal insights.

On the other hand, sometimes it pays to consider a slightly off-beat approach. One thing you might consider is a peer reference from one of your classmates who knows you well and is a good writer. (This type of recommendation is required at Williams College.) Also, don't hesitate to use unconventional references.

Michael Behnke of MIT was much impressed by a letter from a school custodian about how hard an applicant worked with the custodial staff on school projects: "In broken English, the custodian communicated very effectively that this applicant was the only student in the school who paid attention to those who worked in support positions."

Recommendations That Backfired

These two, brought to us by Robert de Veer of Earlham College and Richard Steele of Duke University, must surely rank among the most candid—and most devastating—recommendations of all time.

- Dear Mr. de Veer,
    This applicant lies, cheats and steals. He pesters women and harasses his schoolmates. In my twenty years of teaching here I have never had a worse student. Sincerely yours.
- Dear Mr. Steele:
    Senator ——— [one of the U.S. Senate's most illustrious figures] has been very insistent that I write a letter of recommendation for Julie Jones. I have done so. I know you will know exactly what to do with this letter.

20

SCORING POINTS WITH THE ESSAY

Pity the poor admissions officer, sitting alone in his cramped little office, swamped by a stack of essays six inches thick to read by the end of the day. Boy, are they deadly:

"How My Trip to Europe Changed My Life."

"How I Would Solve World Hunger."

Yawn. Yawn.

Your essay will eventually find its way into that pile, so try to shake the admissions officer out of his stupor and make him notice you. Show him how well you can write and think, and at the same time let him have a peek inside your world. He is interested in learning about you or he wouldn't be in admissions.

THE WRITE STUFF

It helps, of course, if you can write well. As William Buchanan of Virginia Military Institute explains, "The purpose of the VMI essay is to see if the applicant can organize his thoughts and express them in writing."

The sad fact is, most high school students can't write well, and unfortunately, this book can't teach you how. If you doubt your skills, talk it over with your English teacher or get help from your parents or a tutor. (Two good books on the subject are *On Writing Well,* by William Zinsser, and *The Elements of Style,* by William Strunk and E. B. White.)

In the meantime, try to be as concise and specific as possible, and carefully organize your essay around a key theme. Don't waste words that aren't essential to your point, and reread the essay several times for spelling, word choice and typos.

If you have time, put your essay aside for a week or two and then read it again to see if it still makes sense. By choosing your words carefully and proofreading, you show the admissions office not only that you are a good writer, but that you care about the essay and are willing to take the time to do it right.

STRAIGHT FROM THE HEART

That said, we should hasten to add that you don't have to be another Ralph Waldo Emerson to write a good essay. Most admissions offices won't penalize you if there are a few rough edges on your essay—unless, of course, you happen to be applying to places like Harvard or Swarthmore.

The most important thing admissions officers want from the essay is a sense of who you are as a person. "We look for the applicant's voice," says Rick Dalton of Middlebury. It is generally easier to reveal something interesting about yourself if you pick a topic drawn from your own experiences. Don't be shy about showing your unique perspective on something, a relationship perhaps, or explaining an incident that helped you define a value or belief.

Any admissions officer will be impressed if you have the guts to discuss honestly something close to the heart, such as a personal obstacle that you are dealing with or have overcome. John Corso of the University of Tulsa said he was particularly taken with one applicant who wrote his essay about looking in the mirror and reflecting on his homely face, while Anne Price of Lewis and Clark especially liked one girl who wrote as if she were an admissions committee considering her application.

One applicant to Hampden-Sydney College wrote about

a pair of old but treasured shoes he had worn to the interview despite his mother's protests, ending with, "Tell the truth, Dean Jones, did you notice my shoes?" "My response was yes," says Robert Jones, "but it didn't matter. He's a member of the Class of '90."

DON'T TRY TO SAVE THE WORLD

While personal topics usually work well, stay away from intractable political issues, or what Janet Graeter of the State University of New York at Geneseo calls "the social-problem-of-the-year bandwagon."

Essays that are overly self-centered or show insensitivity are also sure to fall flat. "I hated it when an applicant wrote that he had learned from a trip to the ghetto how fortunate he is to live in a nice house," says Richard Wood of Colorado College. A societal problem can occasionally be an interesting topic for an essay, but only if it is done with sensitivity, and only if you can give it a personal slant. For example, lots of people write about the homeless, but one applicant to the University of Miami actually went out and interviewed a homeless man—and was accepted. (See next chapter, "Five Successful Essays.")

In addition to open-ended personal statements, many applications also ask students to answer an essay question. Sooner or later, you may be asked to:

• reflect on an experience that has had a profound impact on your life, and

• discuss the extracurricular activity that was most important to you and explain why.

The most important rule of thumb in cases like these is simple: *Answer the question.* Never, ever substitute the answer to one college's question for that of another unless the two questions are exactly the same.

Another little morsel: If you're doing all your essays on a word processor, for heaven's sake remember to change the name of the college before you print.

Likewise, heed the advice of Roger Campbell of the University of Denver: "Don't send a Xerox copy of your most recent major school paper. We may not agree with your teacher."

IS LAUGHTER THE BEST MEDICINE?

Part of writing a good essay is making yourself memorable, and an obvious way to do it is with a little humor.

Many of the admissions officers we surveyed said they found essays written "with a twinkle in the eye" refreshing, and the Ursinus admissions office won't soon forget the applicant who wrote his on, ahem, sexual fantasies. (He was accepted.)

Be on guard, though, because humor is a double-edged sword that is easy to trip and fall on. "It usually makes the student too casual, too uninterested, and/or flippant," says Richard Hallin of Eckerd College. Only excellent writers should try to be funny, and then only if they can reveal something important about themselves in the process.

As for length, we wholeheartedly recommend the KISS formula of Tim Fuller from Houghton. (Keep It Short and Simple.) Admissions officers reading "their 700th application in two weeks," he says, "are not impressed by long essays."

DON'T LET MOM AND DAD WRITE IT

A final ticklish issue is getting help. There's a fine line between legitimate consultation and illegitimate misrepresentation. The application has your name on it, so the major part of the essay should be your work. It's fine to get a parent or teacher to look it over for spelling and make a comment or two on the content, but if that person begins writing sentences or paragraphs, it isn't your essay anymore.

"I am beginning to see more of the best essays money can buy," says Thomas Pollard of Richmond University, noting the increasing numbers that are ghostwritten. Rest assured, if you got straight Bs in English and your essay reads like E. B. White, the admissions office is going to be skeptical.

The essay is a time to use carefully chosen words to make yourself come alive in the eyes of the admissions office. According to Edward Boehm of Texas Christian University, "The essay is the perfect vehicle for the subtle 'hook'—what sets you apart, distinguishes you from the rest, convinces the committee that you are going to set the campus on fire (figuratively, of course)."

Essay Turnoffs

- *Careless Mistakes.* Do you care about the essay? Then on pain of rejection, correct all your typos, misspelled words and incorrect grammar.
- *Trite Phrases.* Most admissions officers are near nausea with applicants "who want to help people." Think of something that's unique about you.
- *Too Slick.* An essay that reads like it was churned out by Dad's p.r. firm will fall flat. Be genuine. Let the real *you* shine through.
- *Cynicism.* Colleges want bright, active people—not wet blankets. A positive approach to life—and to the essay—will score points.
- *Life Histories.* Make sure your essay has a point. An endless stream of phrases like "then I did this,

and then I did this . . ." is sleep-inducing and doesn't say anything meaningful about you.

- *Too Long.* More is not better. The colleges want a concise, well-reasoned essay—not the sequel to *Gone With the Wind.* Try not to exceed the amount of space allotted for each essay.
- *The Thesaurus Syndrome.* Don't overutilize ostentatiously pretentious language to delineate the subject matter you are attempting to address. Big words aren't impressive; a clear, direct style is.

21

FIVE SUCCESSFUL ESSAYS

Now that you've got an idea of the general do's and don't's for writing your essay, take a look at how six successful applicants completed their assignments. Each of these essays demonstrates an original approach. They are written by ordinary students—presumably, like you. Also included are comments from admissions directors who appreciated them.

UNIVERSITY OF MIAMI
by Kimberly M. Kaplan

As I rest in my warm, cozy, nicely decorated room, equipped with a stereo, television, telephone and much, much more, I have to stop and think, with a tear in both eyes, about the other not-so-fortunate human beings. Especially on this almost freezing night with rain beating on the ground, I try to imagine what it would be like to be without a home, food or a job. Being the sheltered child that I am, I have no clue whatsoever as to how I would feel living in such a deprived situation. Is it fair that I am living in such extreme wealth while there are starving, naked children living on the streets? Is it fair that I have over and above what is needed for a human to survive while there are people begging for a piece of bread? I think those questions would be answered "no" by most people, at least people with hearts.

Mitch Snyder has the heart that the homeless are looking for. He is the hero of the homeless and also a hero of mine and many other people like me. Mitch Snyder, of Washington's Community for Creative Nonviolence, is devoting his whole life to combating the problems of the homeless in our country. He is an individual whose contributions have significantly benefited humanity, and this is why I would nominate him for the Nobel Peace Prize.

Today, I spoke with Mitch Snyder. I found him outside the Capitol Building reading a newspaper sitting underneath a large clear piece of plastic which was keeping him dry from the rain. I found it very hard to interview him for a college application essay while he was speaking of people who can't even get jobs to feed or clothe themselves.

Mitch Snyder is a voice for the others who cannot speak. He believes in creative nonviolence. Protests and fasting are his methods to obtain his goals for the homeless. Mitch Snyder's message that he would like to get across to the public is the ancient saying, "Do unto others as you would have others do unto you." He explains that the homeless want the same things as the rest of the world wants. They would like their own beds in their own rooms. They would like to get the same jobs as the white, middle-class people. He explained to me that a black man, not very well educated, dressed in rags, would not be able to walk into an office and get the same job that a white, middle-class student could get. He clearly stated that he believes there is still a problem with racism.

Overall, I must say that after speaking with Mitch Snyder for two hours, I have been greatly influenced. He has changed the way I feel about myself, and he has expanded my views about our world. The moral values I had yesterday are quite different from today's. I feel that this will give me a chance to make a difference to our community and to myself. I believe that there are many, many other people in our country who have heard Mitch Snyder speak who feel the same way I do. Mitch Snyder not only benefits the homeless, but he is benefiting people in general. Mitch Snyder deserves the recognition of the Nobel Peace Prize.

Comments from Teresa Lahti-Gathje:
"I thought we had read so many 'I will be rich and successful with 2.5 kids' essays that to find someone who admitted she lived in this materialistic world but was still conscious of others who have less shows real maturity. Plus it was a touching essay, and something about it made you think that Kim had real substance."

UNIVERSITY OF MICHIGAN
by J. J. Cromer

Very simply, I love school. I don't mean that I have maroon-and-white rah! rah! Seaholm High blood or anything, but I just get a kick out of going to school.

School is adventure. The crowded hall: a jungle of bodies that even a teenage Tarzan might not conquer. The untouched 2,500-word English paper due next Monday: the seemingly insurmountable Mt. Everest of the high school literary world. The Student Congress meeting: a chance for a bunch of Clark Kents to somehow overcome Superman-like tasks. The soccer game against the state champs: David meets Goliath, revisited. School is my *Star Wars*—the adventures never stop and the deep-down Luke Skywalker in me stands up to face every challenge.

School is people. Freshmen and faculty, sophomores and security guards, juniors and janitors, seniors and secretaries. Together they add up to create the Great Seaholm Melting Pot which I love. I'm friends with a 3.950 MIT-bound math whiz and a 0.395 budding rock star, a girl called "War Rat" and a guy called "The Grunk." Everybody's so different and everybody's so great in their own little (or big) way. I've learned that every single solitary person has something unique and special about them that they can teach everybody else. THAT's why I love dealing with and getting to know so many people: I can learn something from everyone.

Most of all, school is fun. All those people added to all those adventures equals dynamite. As I enter the school every morning, I prepare myself for the best. I might get an A-plus on a calculus test (not likely) or I may share a hilarious story with a good friend at lunch. Whatever the case may be, I feel that the good will always outweigh any bad that may arise. Of course, things never go 100 percent perfectly, but I never expect them to anyway. (Besides, I don't think THAT would be very much fun, either.)

I love high school like a pair of old jeans. Three and a

half years ago, I tried on high school and it was a perfect fit. After a while, jeans become faded and worn—they become personalized. Well, so have my high school years gotten personalized. They sure have made a mark on me and I hope I've made a mark on them. And just like I'll never want to throw out those jeans, I'll never want to throw out my memories of high school.

Comments from Cliff Sjogren:
"After reading this essay, I feel that I almost know Steve. People are important to him, all kinds of people. He has a sense of humor (a most important characteristic for all of us these days!). A clever writer. Certainly not a slick essay—probably written quickly. And it was fun to read."

ROLLINS COLLEGE
by Edward Gibson

I kept wishing that he would get up. I stood in the huddle with my back to him, but I knew he was down. After a moment of forever I heard the crowd cheer and I turned to catch a glimpse of him. Two coaches were carrying number seventy-nine from the field. He limped badly and with his helmet off you could see the pain on his face. Danny, our quarterback, called the play, but I didn't hear it. I went to the line and blocked up high, well away from the knees. I felt our tailback brush off my hip and released my opponent to see what had happened to the ball carrier. He scored, but it didn't matter. All that mattered was that I had intentionally hurt another human. I don't know what happened that day; maybe I was put out with my family and friends or maybe what is buried so deep inside me was suddenly released. I don't know when but at some point during that day I lost my desire to win. All I cared about was defeating the opponent. I wanted to beat them and suppress them and that was the only thing I was playing for. No other desires.

It was a simple but effective play, 22 counter. My block was the key. I was to move laterally along the line of scrimmage past the ball and block the defensive tackle. The play was so effective because the defensive tackle would not be blocked and see the ball carrier coming forward. Caught up in his anxiousness to tackle the ball carrier he would never see me coming. He would be hit from the side; the running back would break off my hip and if all went well make a sizable gain.

"Down!" I put my hand down in a three-point stance and anticipated the count. "Red 9! Red 9!" Anger and disgust for the defensive tackle down the line built up inside of me. "Set!" Go for the knee, humble him, hit where he won't ever get up. "Hut!" Go! Move along the line, I stayed intentionally low, looking for number seventy-nine, the defensive tackle. I found him just as I had expected, standing up, his eyes fixed on our running back. Stay low, I said to myself, and hit hard. I lowered my head and aimed for the side of the knee. My technique was perfect. I was low enough. My right shoulder hit square on its target. All of my strength was channeled up through my legs and it all concentrated into my right shoulder. But when I hit my strength was gone. Not only my physical strength, but my emotional and spiritual as well. All hunger and pride and desire to belittle was gone with the noise. Above the crowd and the clash of pads, above all else was the noise. It sounded like death. It was the loudest noise I have ever heard. It was a crack, not a small one but a loud one. It sounded like a crack that never should have been. It sounded like an oak tree blowing over in the wind. Then came the scream. The tackle was rolling around on the ground. At first, a sense of pride swelled in my throat, but then it died as I realized that I had intentionally injured him and I was ashamed.

I have never looked at sports or life quite the same. It is no longer important to me to gain at another's losses. I am no longer concerned with being better than the rest. Only with being better.

Comments from David Erdmann:

"This student seems humbled by the experience he described. He is, it seems to us, a better person as a result of that experience, and we not only applaud him for his recognition and appreciation of humility but also believe he will enter our institution with a finely tuned concern for others."

DUKE UNIVERSITY
by Catherine Vorland Laskey

The invention of the SAT has had a significant influence on the lives of college-bound teenagers during the twentieth century. A student's first encounter with this dreaded exam haunts him until he has finally been accepted by a college. The clock ticking and his heart throbbing, the SAT victim is crouched over his desk, concentrating with the utmost prudence on each question. Because a high score on this exam is a criterion for his admission to the college of his choice, he is anxious and strained. Will he run out of time? Will the correct answers escape him? Will the college accept his score? Those three hours of grueling toil branded an indelible impression on my mind and on the minds of the rest of my generation. I left the exam room thinking:

> How may I test thee? Let me count the ways.
> I test thee with the math and the verbal
> Until thy mind is likened to a gerbil's
> And all colleges know and sing thy praise.
> (apologies to Elizabeth Barrett Browning)

Most high school juniors and seniors endure the three hours of Sadistic Aptitude Torture only to be stamped with a Dow Jones verbal and math aptitude score. The number one receives from the testing service is one to be committed to memory along with one's Tillie the Teller code number, one's Social Security number, and the phone number of the nearest Domino's pizza.

Recently, there has been a flurry of excitement among the nation's schools over current reports indicating an increase in national scores, the first since 1963. I say that JFK's spirit must somehow be hovering over American high schools wailing: "Ask not what you can do for your school, ask what your school can do for your score." (The *National Enquirer* may quote me.)

The SAT tests a student's analytical math skills including the ability to convert word problems into math symbols and math symbols into words. Typically, the word problems reign supreme with some seeming as absurd as the following:

Ships A and B are traveling at speed X. If ice cubes are added to the pool of ship A, do the shivering passengers:

    (a) increase
    (b) decrease
    (c) take hot showers
    (d) drink warm tea
    (e) jump ship

The correct response (d) would be logically deduced by the student with the strong math background who is able to determine that all the ice is in the pool and thus cannot be used for drinks. That requires math intuition, just what colleges are looking for in their students.

Once past the math sections, the student encounters the verbal challenges of which the obscure analogy question is always heartening:

    zucchetto: yarmulke
    (a) shoe: toe
    (b) air: eggs
    (c) burrito: enchilada
    (d) floor: pool
    (e) school: prison

One zeroes in on the correct answer (c) immediately if one is the incomparable English student who, yes, has his dictionary memorized.

The sentence completion question follows, which always seems to have more than one best response:

Although the armadillo was respected by his peer group, his recent actions were not considered ———.

  (a) proper
  (b) suitable
  (c) appropriate
  (d) apropros
  (e) compatible

The whim of the test creator decides the correct reply, and, of course, he gives the student a generous one out of five chances of guessing accurately.

The verbal portion generally concludes with a reading comprehension section wherein lengthy passages on the lifestyle of the zooid and its compeers are followed by two to five pertinent questions about the author's implications.

Bearing in mind that approximately one and a half million students annually take the SAT offers some solace to the SAT victim. After all, to quote a trite maxim, "misery loves company."

So here we are, almost two million of us, with our four years of high school knowledge reduced to a mere three- or four-digit number that signifies nothing but how well we have endured three hours of Sadistic Aptitude Torture. In order to maintain some semblance of sanity and prevent an epidemic of ulcers in teenagers, we must reflect on our situation in a lighthearted vein. Only with this sense of humor can we bear the pressures and trials of the life ahead of us.

Comments from Richard Steele:
"This essay is one of the best I have read in years. Why? First, it is witty, cleverly developed and very original. Second, it really does reveal a lot about this candidate's character and ability. She is a gifted writer, she has a wonderful sense of humor, and she has retained

*much of what she has read. In reading this essay it
becomes obvious that she has read widely (note her reference to Browning, the* National Enquirer *and J.F.K.'s
speech). Her choice of topic (mocking the importance of
the SAT) reveals that this student is a risk-taker. Her
treatment of that subject makes it clear that she has a
lively mind and that she can organize her thoughts very
effectively. These two pages convinced me that she is
bright, interesting, witty and likable—an ideal student
for Duke."*

DAVIDSON COLLEGE
by Brad Grayson

They were after me. As fast as I ran, one of them was
always close behind.

I heard the report and ducked instinctively, feeling the
air part as a Misspelling flew over my head. "They" were
SAs, terrifying creatures who were intrinsic to the college
admission process. Their only goal was to be "Completed," something that prospective students wanted to
do. However, this required extensive thought and expres-
sive writing, and with the forces of procrastination and
laziness as allies, applicants were forced to put up a tough
battle.

I could tell that this particular SA was not going to
yield without a fight. I raced down the corridors, past
the stacks of rejected essays, and finally gained a clear
shot. I hit it with a Service Club. The SA parried the
blow with a Vague and retaliated with a Deadwood. I
knew then that I was in trouble; this SA had to be from
one of those "Most Competitive" schools, from the way
it shrugged off my blows. Most likely it was a Davidson
SA, judging from the looks of the mini-SAs that were
homing in on me.

I dispatched the first with an Achievement Theme, but the second mini caught me with a vicious Honor Code Query. I countered this with a Real-Life Experience, then turned to face the third mini-SA. However, this one was not to be denied, and wrapped me up in a Significant Contribution that sent me reeling. Just then the major SA captured me and I was carried off for the ultimate test: Completion.

For some, Completion is simply a matter of sitting down and writing. However, if you are like me, thoughts come freely and sometimes unorganized, and assembling them takes time. Often they must be forced out, and this was what the SA was in the process of doing.

Its sharp, probing questions stung. "Tell me about yourself," it demanded. "What are you like?" it asked. It was too much, and I begged for release. "I'll tell you anything," I said.

The thoughts came tumbling out: likes surfing . . . reading . . . works at the Chart House Restaurant . . . outwardly tough, inwardly compassionate . . . enjoys traveling . . . drives a '77 station wagon . . . terminal procrastinator . . . five-year Latin student . . . sings in the shower . . . likes to be with people . . . favorite author is Larry Niven . . . loves water sports . . . sees architecture as a possible career . . . arguments with my dad . . . sleeping late on Saturdays . . . my German shepherd . . . my messy room . . . endless essays in AP English . . . loves boating . . . waterskiing . . . likes to dance . . . going to Burger King for lunch . . . wanting to go to Davidson . . .

Within minutes, the SA squeezed out all of the meaningful facts about me and presented me with my orders: Complete before Deadline, or suffer Rejection.

Now, if there is one thing that students avoid more than Completion, it is the fear of Rejection. I certainly did not want to fall prey to this ignominious ending to my college dreams.

Armed with this previously hidden knowledge, I banished Procrastination and laughed at the conquered SA. I knew that I could abate the agony of Completion, because it was all in my mind.

Behind me, the SA faded away. After all, how hard is it to write about yourself if you have all the facts?

Comments from Robert E. Gardner:
This essay is "insightful, clever, thoughtful, well executed—in short, it reflects significant effort and a personal perspective rare among seventeen-year-olds."

22

FOOTING THE BILL

Let's play a guessing game. How much do you think four years at a top private college will cost you and your family?

(a) $40,000
(b) $60,000
(c) $75,000
(d) $1,000,000

If you guessed $40,000, you're living in the dark ages; gas was fifty cents a gallon back then. If you guessed $60,000, you're closer but still too low.

The correct answer is about $75,000. That's right, assuming today's prices with modest annual increases, it'll take about $75,000 to pay for four years at a top private college including tuition, fees, and housing. Got any bright ideas on how to pay for it?

START BY TALKING IT OVER WITH YOUR PARENTS

Your parents are the ones who are probably going to foot the lion's share of the bill, so before your college search gets very far, you ought to have a talk with them about finances. (We recommend the winter of your junior year.) Even if you're looking at relatively inexpensive schools, college will be a major investment.

PRICE VS. COST

After your talk, start looking into some strategies to meet your goals. The guidance office is the best place to begin. Your counselor can tell you what other students have done to make ends meet, as well as give some good sources of information for scholarships. (See Chapter 6, "Recommended Reading.") He or she might even be able to provide a list of organizations that might give you some money if you asked.

Don't be worried if at first glance some of the schools you're interested in seem out of your price range. Just because a college has a "sticker price" of $15,000 doesn't mean you'll actually have to pay that much.

"The most common mistake families make is dismissing college choices on the basis of 'price' without researching financial aid, scholarship and other financing options," says James Reilly of Ripon College. Only after all your offers for financial aid have come in should finances enter the picture. There are literally dozens of potential sources of aid available which every smart family—no matter what its financial situation—can take advantage of.

There are two types of financial aid: need-based and merit.

NEED-BASED FINANCIAL AID

What You Need Is What You Get. The more expensive the school, the more need-based financial aid it is likely to give out. This aid comes in three forms: grants, loans and work-study jobs. In order to qualify, you must fill out the College Board's Financial Aid Form (FAF), or American College Testing Program's Family Financial Statement (FFS). (Which one you need to complete depends on the school.)

These forms in turn determine your family's expected contribution. This figure is subtracted from the cost of the particular institution to determine the amount of aid for which you qualify. If you are very needy, most of your aid will be in the form of grants. In general, needs of roughly $3,000 per year or less are met with loans and work-study, and anything beyond that in grants. Be careful, though, because no college is required to meet your "demonstrated need." Some make it a policy to meet a fixed proportion, such as 90 percent of need, and even those that guarantee 100 percent often vary the proportion of grants and loans. Students they are eager to attract will be offered this aid in the form of outright grants rather than loans that must be repaid.

But Will It Affect My Chances? There is good news and bad news here. The good news is that at most of the very top schools, admissions is *need-blind*—that is, your ability to pay has no effect on your chances. The bad news is that not every school is rich enough to have this policy.

Few schools relish the idea of rejecting people because they can't afford to pay, but the fact is that sometimes finances play a role in admissions decisions. Some schools admit needy students until their financial aid money runs out—and then give preference to those who can pay—while others admit students with an "unmet need" the students must somehow make up. Before you apply, check the policies of the schools that interest you.

MERIT SCHOLARSHIPS

Where the Bucks Are. With colleges eager to attract the best students, many schools have turned to merit scholarships to help them lure the cream of the crop. These range from token grants of a few hundred dollars to all-expense-paid free rides. Find out whether the colleges you're interested in offer them.

In addition to the colleges, innumerable foundations and corporations sponsor scholarships. The best known of these is the College Board's National Merit Scholarship program, which awards nearly 4,500 scholarships every year based primarily on PSAT scores.

Fraternal organizations like the American Legion and

the Rotary Club are also fertile sources of aid. Indeed, there are so many private companies and organizations that offer scholarships that the main problem is sifting through them all to find the right ones for you.

Getting Your Hands on It. The conventional strategy is to camp out in the guidance office and pore over books of listings. (See Chapter 6, "Recommended Reading.")

Another alternative is scholarship search services, which for a fee of about forty dollars will scan a computer data base and spit out a list of about ten scholarships that might be right for you. Most of these organizations appear to be aboveboard, but their data bases are notoriously inconsistent and often out-of-date. Before you sign up with one, check with your counselor to see if he or she has ever found one to be useful.

Last, find out if the places where Mom and Dad work have a tuition-abatement program. Many organizations will help pay the college costs of the children of their employees.

Computer Search Services: Do They Really Work?

Some do, but others look suspiciously like rip-offs. So before you sign up with any service, comparison-shop with the following questions in mind:

- *How much will it cost me?* The standard price is about $40.
- *How many sources are in the company's data base?* This number should be well into the thousands.
- *How often is the data base updated?* A good one will be updated at least once a year.
- *How successful have past participants been?* You're unlikely to get a firm figure. Evaluate whatever evidence the company presents.
- *Is there a minimum number of sources I will get?* Be skeptical of any number less than ten.
- *Can I get my money back if I'm not satisfied?* Many firms will give refunds, but with strings attached. Read the fine print.

The answers to these questions should separate the phonies from the real thing. Unfortunately, we can't give you any hard and fast rules, so you'll have to use common sense. If for, say, $40 you think a search service can give you an outside chance of finding a scholarship, it might be worth it. Hitting the jackpot, after all, could mean thousands of dollars.

THE GOVERNMENT

Federal Funds and State Subsidies. Here is a chance for your parents to get back some of the money they have been giving to Uncle Sam all these years. Even financially secure families may be eligible for Guaranteed Student Loans or PLUS parent loans, which can provide up to $3,000 dollars a year at reasonable interest rates. Many state governments also offer grants and/or loans for college. For more information, talk to your counselor or get in touch with your state and local governments.

For students who don't mind a stint in the military after graduation, signing up for the Reserve Officers Training Corps (ROTC) can mean thousands of dollars in extra money for college.

DO IT NOW

As with picking a college, the golden rule in financial aid is *start early*. The longer you look for money, the better the odds that you'll find it.

23

THE BEST COLLEGE BARGAINS

Everyone knows that the cost of a college education is soaring. That's the bad news.

The good news is that *some* colleges have been winning the battle against above-inflation price increases. For write-ups on more than 200 such colleges, go to any good bookstore and get a copy of *Best Buys in College Education*, written by Edward B. Fiske and Joseph M. Michalak and published by Times Books.

In the meantime, here is a list of the best bargains in American education—categorized by what enables them to keep tuition down.

COLLEGES WITH LARGE ENDOWMENTS:

> Baylor University, Texas
> Butler University, Indiana
> Cooper Union, New York
> Deep Springs College, California (two-year)
> Rice University, Texas
> Southwestern University, Texas
> Wabash College, Indiana

COLLEGES WITH CHURCH SUBSIDIES:

> Brigham Young University, Utah
> University of Dallas, Texas
> Luther College, Iowa
> St. Olaf College, Minnesota
> Wheaton College, Illinois

WELL-MANAGED INSTITUTIONS:

> Birmingham-Southern College, Alabama
> Centre College, Kentucky
> Cornell College, Iowa
> Grove City College, Pennsylvania
> Oglethorpe University, Georgia
> University of Puget Sound, Washington
> Rose-Hulman Institute of Technology, Indiana

LEADING COLLEGES IN AREAS OF THE COUNTRY WHERE THE COST OF LIVING IS LOW:

Hendrix College, Arizona
Millsaps College, Michigan
Trinity University, Texas
University of Tulsa, Oklahoma

COLLEGES WHERE ALL STUDENTS WORK TO KEEP EXPENSES DOWN:

Berea College, Kentucky
Blackburn College, Illinois
Drexel University, Pennsylvania
Northeastern University, Massachusetts

PUBLICS THAT OFFER THE FLAVOR OF A PRIVATE LIBERAL ARTS COLLEGE:

State University of New York at Geneseo
University of Minnesota at Morris
New College of the University of South Florida
St. Mary's College of Maryland
Shepherd College, West Virginia

24

GIMMICKS

Were you thinking you'd like to add something a little out of the ordinary to your application package? Do you want to capture the admissions committee's attention, distinguish yourself from every Tom, Dick and Harriet who applies?

It doesn't take admissions directors long to recall at least one applicant who won them over by daring to be different and adding zest to the sometimes mundane selection process. As long as you realize that a gimmick won't rescue you at a school you're not academically qualified for, you could certainly employ a tactful one to make a bold case for your acceptance.

The gimmick is different from the hook (see Chapter 11, "By Hook or by Crook") because it's not the presentation of an inherited characteristic or an established talent. Rather, a gimmick demonstrates your creative ability to tackle a new project—the college application process—in an imaginative fashion.

For example, one student, who will not soon be forgotten at Texas Christian University, sent a sample of his own company's product—a Nativity scene made of chocolate. Such cleverness and ingenuity may be just what a college is seeking in members of its next freshman class. On the other hand, a meaningless, cutesy plea for attention comes up a *reject* every time.

Here are some that fell into this category:

• One applicant to Le Moyne College sent the admissions director's wife a dozen roses and put an advertisement in the paper pleading his case for acceptance. Sorry, Charlie.

• A young woman sent an 8-by-10 glossy of herself in a baton-twirling outfit and left her application blank, simply stating that she wanted to be admitted. The admissions director assumed the applicant thought the picture "said it all." It didn't.

Another unsuccessful candidate thrust a portfolio of her "cheesecake" modeling photographs on an admissions director. He was not impressed.
• Then there's the student applying to St. John's College (New Mexico) who completed his application in poetic form on the back of matchbook covers. So what?

Now, just to get your creative juices flowing, consider the following true-life examples of *successful* gimmicks:
• One applicant with a well-thought-out plan developed a company letterhead and wrote as if he were an alumnus, president of the company and an international business leader willing to contribute to his alma mater. Only in the P.S. did he disclose that he was a freshman applicant demonstrating how things could be ten years from now if he were admitted. He was.

This student was successful because he made a statement about his goals and the role that a college education would play in the attainment of those goals. The philosophy here is that once you've gotten an admissions director to notice you, you'd better have something to show for yourself.
• Another applicant presented his case via his 100-pound basset hound. He used ten or so photographs of his dog, and each one gave some significant commentary about him as a master. This presentation was not only eye-catching, but it also said something about him as a considerate and caring person.
• One student who was wait-listed at Worcester Polytechnic Institute wrote, typeset and had printed a two-color, four-page brochure promoting himself. He didn't have to wait on their list for long.

Positive attributes presented in a novel but tactful way are the only "gimmicks" that admissions directors are buying. Note what Elizabeth Donaghey of the University of Lowell says: "The sincere person stands a better chance than some handshaking, baby-kissing salesman." But remember that there's no reason why a sincere, likable person can't distinguish himself from the masses.

N.AKGULIAN

25

THIN LETTERS AND FAT

For high school seniors, April is mail-watching month. You can usually tell the moment you lift a college admissions office envelope from the mailbox if it carries tidings of great joy or cause for major depression.

Meaty envelopes are stuffed with cordial letters of acceptance and information about enrollment and freshman housing.

Skinny envelopes hold nothing more than a "Dear John" letter or notification that you have been placed on a waiting list.

Every day your high school buzzes with gossip of who was accepted or rejected where. Your relatives keep calling to see if you've heard any news yet. The tension mounts. Your nerves become frazzled. You begin to believe your destiny is tied to the weight of your mail. And you're certain that if the "best" school rejects you, you'll be an all-time loser.

WAIT A MINUTE

First of all, if you've followed the advice of this book, you haven't put all your hopes and dreams into one admissions basket. If you've done your homework, you know that there's more than one college for you.

Never take a college rejection personally. It doesn't necessarily mean your academic record is inadequate. It just tells you there wasn't a slot that you could fill, for whatever reason—rational or irrational. (See Chapter 2, "The Poker Game.")

NOBODY'S PERFECT

No matter how well admissions officers know their schools and the mixture of students they're seeking, they do make mistakes. And although it's a rare occurrence, they have been known to reverse their decisions.

A blanket recommendation of "if at first you don't get in, appeal, appeal again" is not the answer to every college turn-down. But there might be an instance where you are genuinely shocked by a rejection because your credentials are as good or better than most students admitted. Or maybe you realize, after the fact, that you left out some valuable explanatory information about your background that would have helped the admissions committee get to know you, the Person, as opposed to you, the Application File. In cases such as these, a polite and properly executed appeal might be in order.

AN ACCEPTANT TO EVERY RULE

But one football player who was rejected from Wabash College because of his less-than-impressive academic record is living proof that miracles do happen. This young man reapplied to Wabash and asked that he be interviewed by several faculty members and members of the admissions committee. He sold them in person and was admitted. "He simply had a goal and wasn't going to be denied," says the admissions director, Cal Black.

PROPER APPEAL ETIQUETTE

Following are some do's and don't's for appealing decisions:

• DON'T call up the admissions office ranting and raving about being treated unfairly.

• DO compose a well-written, logical letter expressing your sincere disappointment in having been rejected, and explain in precise terms why you still believe this is the right school for you.

• DO provide any formerly left out information that supports your argument.

• DO request an interview with someone in the admissions office if you haven't already had one.

• DON'T get your hopes up too much. Appeals rarely work.

HANDLING THE WAIT LIST

The waiting list is a different story—and a growing phenomenon. With more and more students submitting multiple applications, colleges are less and less sure about how many applicants will be accepting their offers of admission. The way they hedge their bets is to create large waiting lists. When you're on one, you have no idea how close you are to admittance. About the only thing you do know is that you haven't been rejected—yet.

BETTER SAFE THAN SORRY

If you are wait-listed, do yourself a favor and send a deposit to your first choice of the schools that accepted you. In other words, don't stake your college career on the hope that you'll get into Wait List U. Some schools compile wait lists of more than a thousand students; highly selective schools frequently don't need to accept a single student from their wait lists.

But according to admission directors, persistence and continued demonstration of your earnest desire to attend can sometimes help you move up the wait list. If you find yourself wait-listed at one of your first-choice colleges, don't just sit back and hope for fat mail; take action.

• Send an ever-so-polite letter ASAP to the admissions director emphasizing your unyielding desire to attend. Many colleges consider only those students who respond in writing that they would accept an offer of admission. So let the admissions office know that they can count on you.

• Make some follow-up phone calls, and keep inquiring as to the status of the wait list. Make plans to visit the college and politely inquire about getting an interview to plead your case.

• Ask your guidance counselor if he or she can call or write the admissions office on your behalf.

• Be sure that the college is kept up-to-date about any honors or achievements since you filed your application.

Little Things Can Be Important

At Bucknell University, one wait-listed student whose last name began with a Z sent the admissions office an imaginative letter in which he explained how he had always been at the end of the line alphabetically, causing him anxiety and frustration. He politely asked the admissions committee not to approach their waiting list alphabetically. "His well-written letter, and the good humor reflected in that letter, resulted in his being placed near the top of the waiting list. The student was subsequently admitted, and graduated with significant accomplishment," says Richard Skelton.

DON'T LET TURN-DOWNS GET YOU DOWN

If you're not on a waiting list, and you've been irreversibly rejected by your top-priority schools, don't dwell on the negative. "Take the college admissions process seriously but please don't let it get you down. There are dozens of excellent choices for you," says Joseph Carver of Babson College.

Begin to focus your attention on the schools that did accept you. Think about why the admissions committees at these colleges thought you would be a good match. What was it about you that they liked and appreciated that the other schools didn't commend? If you can answer this question, you might find the best reason to attend.

As Kevin Rooney of the University of Notre Dame explains, "Students should take comfort in the fact that most of the professionals who assist students and parents in the process are dedicated to the best match between students and institution. I believe that most students find their way to a suitable college or university."

How Not to Appeal a College Rejection

The mother of a student denied admission to Rutgers University made an impassioned plea over the phone for her son, alleging that his poor record was the result of her marital troubles and divorce. "Clearly, the young man, of average ability to begin with, had consistently done the minimum required of him in school," says Evelyn Finck, the admissions director. "I said, 'Frankly, Mrs. Jones, I don't think your divorce had a thing to do with his record.' She replied, 'You're right—the little s---!'"

26

SOME THOUGHTS FOR PARENTS

This book is directed primarily at students, who are herewith invited to skip to the next chapter. Parents may read on.

Choosing a college is often the first time that the young person is making a major decision on his or her own. It is, as Phil Smith of Williams puts it, "the first time in the child-parent relationship that parents don't call the shots."

This means that some tensions between parent and child are understandable, perhaps even likely. It also means, however, that picking a college can be a growing experience—one that broadens the students' horizons, stirs their powers of observation and creativity, and gives them valuable experience in grown-up decision-making.

WHO'S GOING TO COLLEGE ANYWAY?

Young people still seeking to figure out who they are are readily confused by conflicting pressures from peers, teachers, counselors and even colleges themselves. The last thing they need is more agenda items from their own parents. Unfortunately, admissions directors tell us, this is frequently what happens.

The worst difficulties arise with parents who are living their own lives through their offspring or, as one counselor put it, "trying to fix their own broken dreams through their children." Says William Hiss of Bates, "My heart goes out to those youngsters whose parents are trying to pressure their children into a 'name institution' to boost their own egos."

A sure sign that parents have wrapped their own egos into their child's application is the "misplaced we" that shows up in interviews. "We were ranked third in the state in fourteen-and-under women's singles." That, says Tim Fuller of Houghton College, is why admissions officers have swivel chairs—"so they can physically turn away from pushy parents during an interview."

A related problem comes with parents who themselves have been academically or professionally successful. "I see parents who have rarely had to take no for an answer and so find it impossible to take no for an answer when their daughter is not offered admission," says Lynette Robinson-Weening of Simmons College. "I see parents who figure that they can manipulate the system to make it work for their kid, no matter what the cost. Somewhere in all that is a seventeen- or eighteen-year old, trying to figure out what is best."

High school seniors remain sensitive to parental expectations. "Our children know how we feel," wrote the counselors at Weston High School in Connecticut in a recent message to the parents of seniors. "They know what we treasure, what we believe and what we expect of and hope for them." They are well aware of parental attitudes toward the selection of a college and tend to see their acceptance or rejection at particular institutions as "the most important judgments that will ever be made about them" and even as a signal of "whether or not they have fulfilled our hopes and our aspirations." This, noted the counselors, "is pressure few of us have ever experienced."

Pursued with mutual respect and seasoned with a large shaker of common sense, the college search can be one that enriches both students and parents.

HOW TO BE HELPFUL

Parents play an important role in the college search process—functioning at various times as tour directors, cheerleaders, cattle prods, crying towels and general traveling companions on the road to finding the right college or university. How they fulfill these various roles can do much to determine whether the journey will be bumpy or smooth.

Following are some navigational aids for dads and moms of college applicants:

Be Consistent. "Don't switch gears on your son or daughter," says Lois Conrad of Tulane University. "If they did their homework without your nagging, don't start nagging now about applying to college. If you had to push for homework, you'll have to push for applications to get done. Be consistent with your own previous parenting of them."

Communicate. One of the most important things that parents can do is push their sons and daughters to think through the basic questions. Why do you want to go to college? What are your most important needs and goals? What kind of college will best serve them? Communicating with an adolescent is not always easy, but look for the moments that present themselves. Being available to talk when your child has a question or wants to express an idea or feeling is one of the most important and effective things you can do.

Be Realistic. Don't set your child up for failure by encouraging unrealistic applications. Look honestly at your child's academic record. Then study the admissions criteria of colleges that show up on your lists and check out the profiles of the last freshman class. If he or she is not Stanford material, don't swing by Palo Alto on your college tour.

Don't end up like the distraught mother who was shocked to learn from an admissions officer that her son's grades precluded him from being a viable candidate. "I knew Trevor wasn't in the *top* half of his class," she said, "but no one told me he was in the *bottom* half."

Think Broadly. The United States has the most diverse system of higher education anywhere in the world. As we've said several times in this book, there are scores of colleges that would be a good match for every student. You are probably in a better position than your son or daughter to understand this and to get away from what Ronald Potier of Franklin and Marshall College calls the "brand-name syndrome—if people haven't heard of it, it can't be any good."

Set Your Child Up for Success. Make it one of your tasks to be sure that your son or daughter applies to at least two colleges where he or she will definitely be accepted. Then even the worst-case scenario will still be a happy one. As Rick Dalton of Middlebury puts it, "Having the opportunity to choose rather than having to settle on one college begins the college relationship on a better footing."

Whatever Happens, Be Supportive. As the process unfolds, remind your children that they will be accepted at a good school—one where they will make friends, have fun, be challenged and get the education they seek and deserve. When the decisions are in, redouble your efforts on this score and, if necessary, remind them of the fickle nature of the whole selection process.

Perhaps the Weston counselors put it best: "We should help them understand that we love and care for them no matter what a given college decides," they wrote. "We need to make it clear to them that college admission decisions are NOT evaluations of them either as students or as valuable human beings. Let them know that, no matter what, you believe they are unique individuals whom you love and respect."

27

A FINAL WORD
TO STUDENTS

Contrary to what many people would have you believe, deciding on which college to attend is not the most important decision that you will ever make. It's a significant decision, one that should be approached with care and deliberation. But it should be kept in perspective.

For one thing, recognize that there is no single "right" college for you or anyone else. There are scores—probably hundreds—of schools where you will fit in and get a good education. If you follow the principles discussed in the preceding pages, you will find yourself in one of them. It probably doesn't even make a whole lot of difference whether it's one of your top choices.

"College is a wonderful experience," says Ann Quinley of the University of Connecticut. "Whatever disappointments the application process brings, for the vast majority of students six weeks into the freshman year they won't be able to *imagine* they ever could have gone anywhere else."

Selecting a college is a chance to travel, meet new people, test your aspirations and get a glimpse of the challenges that lie before you, says Lorraine Zimmer of Ursinus College. "If you approach it as an adventure, you can get an education just looking for your next place to get an education."

So relax and make a conscious decision to enjoy the process of looking for a college. "The whole thing should be fun," says Thomas Anthony of Colgate University. "If it isn't, then something impractical, unrealistic or unreasonable is being injected. Time to step back and try again." Keep a sense of humor even when things seem to be going wrong. "When you are nervous and only seventeen years old," says Lorna Blake of Smith College, "just about anything is forgivable."

Finally, realize that the college search is the opening act of what Ms. Quinley called that "wonderful experience." Your four years at college will equip you with some marketable skills—or at least with the ability to develop such skills in a field that requires graduate study. But this is only part of the value of college. The real values are personal.

Abraham Lincoln was riding through New Jersey on a train once when someone pointed out that he was passing by Rutgers College. He looked out the window and re- marked, "One of the greatest regrets of my life is that I did not receive a college education." The real value of spending four years in a rich academic environment rests in what it does for you as an individual—in expanding your horizons, in putting what you know in historical, social and other kinds of perspective, in introducing you to the great artists and thinkers who have shaped our world.

In one of his final reports as president of Yale Univer- sity, Kingman Brewster, Jr., described the value of a lib- eral arts education, and we can think of no better way to sum up what lies down the road on which you are now embarking than to remember his words.

"The most fundamental value of a liberal education," he said, "is that it makes life more interesting. This is true whether you are fetched up on a desert island or adrift in the impersonal loneliness of the urban hurly- burly. It allows you to see things which the under- educated do not see. It allows you to understand things which the untutored find incomprehensible. It allows you to think things which do not occur to the less learned. In short, it makes it less likely that you will be bored with life. It also makes it less likely that you will be a crashing bore to those whose company you keep."

WHAT TO DO WHEN

JUNIOR YEAR

September–December
Begin sizing yourself up and reading college guides. Meet with guidance counselor. Take PSAT.

January–March
Sift through college-search mail. Begin preliminary winnowing. Consider SAT prep course and register for May or June test date, or register for ACT if applicable. Talk to parents, teachers and older friends about colleges they know about that may interest you. Discuss finances and college selection process with parents and begin investigating scholarship opportunities. Register for AP tests.

April
Meet with guidance counselor to discuss list of fifteen or twenty schools. Begin planning summer visits. Continue research and begin to dig deeper. Prepare to take SAT or ACT. If you are interested in Early Decision or Early Action, you should take the appropriate test by June.

May
Take SAT if scheduled. Settle on list of eight to twelve to visit and begin planning trips. Take AP Tests.

June
Take SAT or ACT if scheduled. Relax and enjoy the end of school.

July–August
Go on summer visits. Drop and add schools from your list. Talk with friends about schools they are interested in.

SENIOR YEAR

September

Continue visits. Meet with counselor. Consider Early Decision or Early Action if you have taken the SAT or ACT in the preceding spring. Arrange to take SAT, ACT and/or Achievement Tests in October, November or December. Continue scholarship search.

October

Begin filling out applications, continue visits. Settle on final list of five to eight schools to apply to. Take ACT if scheduled. Get a copy of your transcript and check it over. Talk with your counselor about the logistics of the application process. Give out recommendation forms if applying Early Decision. Double-check deadlines for admission, housing and financial aid. Schedule alumni interviews (if applicable).

November

Take SAT, or Achievement Tests if scheduled. File Early Decision or Early Action application depending on deadline. Give out recommendation forms for schools with January regular admission deadlines. Continue working on applications.

December

Take SAT or Achievement Tests if scheduled. File applications with January deadlines. Politely check with teachers and counselor to make sure that recommendations and transcript have been sent.

January–March

Continue to fill out applications and follow up. Take last SAT, ACT or Achievement Tests. Register for AP Tests. Have your parents fill out the College Board Financial Aid Form (FAF) or College Search Service Family

Financial Statement (FFS), depending on which the schools you apply to require. File it as soon as possible.

April

Receive decision letters. Make last-minute visits to colleges that accept you. Make final decision and send in deposit. Scrutinize financial aid package and call the college if you have a concern.

May

Take AP Test. Give yourself a pat on the back. You did it!

APPLICANTS' RIGHTS AND OBLIGATIONS

When students pick a college they are in fact buying a "product" called education. Colleges, in turn, are selling this same product.

In 1987 the College Board published what amounts to a bill of rights and responsibilities for "consumers" of higher education. The title is "Guidelines on Fair Admissions Practices," and it may be obtained free of charge by writing the College Board, 45 Columbus Ave., New York, N.Y. 10023–6992. Following are some of the key guidelines:

COLLEGES HAVE A RESPONSIBILITY TO:

1. Publish their admissions policies.
2. Describe their admissions criteria and provide applicants with sufficient information to "make a reasonable estimate of the likelihood of their meeting their standards."
3. Give applicants the chance to explain "why their academic records may not adequately represent their abilities."
4. State publicly "whether or not their policies include consideration of nonacademic qualities."
5. Provide students denied admission with "a statement of the general reasons for rejection."
6. Give rejected applicants an opportunity for "personal inquiry" into their situation.

APPLICANTS HAVE A RESPONSIBILITY TO:

1. Research and observe the "deadlines, restrictions and fees" of institutions to which they apply.
2. Submit materials "completely, accurately and within the specified deadlines."

3. Confirm at "only one" college or university their intention to enroll.

4. Notify other institutions that have offered admission that they will not be enrolling.

5. Inform colleges of any "unusual circumstances regarding their application and potential enrollment."

COLLEGE TRIVIA

Anyone for a little serendipity? In the pages that follow, we offer you a smorgasbord of information that we uncovered about colleges while compiling this book. Since there is no particular rhyme or reason to the lists reproduced here, we recommend that you simply browse through and read whichever ones strike your fancy. Whether you want to know which colleges have produced the most Rhodes Scholars, or where one can major in psycholinguistics, we hope you will find this compilation of trivia both entertaining and informative.

COLLEGES ENROLLING THE MOST NATIONAL MERIT SCHOLARS IN THE CLASS OF 1990

1. Harvard University (297)
2. Yale University (183)
3. Stanford University (172)
4. Princeton University (140)
5. Massachusetts Institute of Technology (108)
6. Duke University (83)
7. University of Michigan (78)
8. Cornell University (68)
9. University of California at Berkeley (62)
10. University of Virginia (62)

SOURCE: National Merit Scholarship Corporation as cited in *The Chronicle of Higher Education,* April 8, 1987. The figures do not include scholars sponsored by the colleges themselves.

COLLEGES PRODUCING THE MOST NATIONAL SCIENCE FOUNDATION GRADUATE FELLOWS

1. California Institute of Technology
2. Swarthmore College
3. Harvey Mudd College
4. Massachusetts Institute of Technology
5. Princeton University
6. Harvard University
7. Reed College
8. University of Chicago

9.   Yale University
10.   Pomona College

SOURCE: *Science* magazine, July 1986. The data is for the years 1976 to 1983. The fellowships are awarded to first-year graduate students in the sciences who have outstanding undergraduate records. Approximately 500 are awarded each year in a highly competitive selection process.

MOST RHODES SCHOLARS EVER*

Harvard University	228
Yale University	170
Princeton University	160
United States Military Academy	61
Stanford University	53
Dartmouth College	52
University of Virginia	39
Brown University	33
University of Washington	31
Reed College	29
United States Naval Academy	29

*The scholarships were first awarded in 1903.

SOURCE: Office of the American Secretary, Rhodes Scholarship Program, Pomona College, Claremont, California.

MOST RHODES SCHOLARS SINCE 1980

Harvard University	32
Princeton University	22
Yale University	19
Stanford University	13
United States Air Force Academy	8
United States Naval Academy	7
Cornell University	5
Georgetown University	5
Michigan State University	5
Carleton College	4
Columbia University	4

Dartmouth College   4
Tulane University   4

SOURCE: Office of the American Secretary, Rhodes Scholarship Program, Pomona College, Claremont, California.

COLLEGES ENROLLING THE MOST FOREIGN STUDENTS

University of Southern California	3,700
University of Texas at Austin	3,100
University of Wisconsin at Madison	2,900
Columbia University	2,700
Ohio State University	2,700
Boston University	2,500
University of California at Los Angeles	2,500
University of Minnesota	2,500
University of Houston	2,400
University of Michigan at Ann Arbor	2,400

SOURCE: Institute of International Education, New York City.

COLLEGES WITH THE HIGHEST PERCENTAGE OF FOREIGN STUDENTS

University of San Francisco	25%
Howard University	20%
Massachusetts Institute of Technology	19%
American University	16%
Southern University A&M, Los Angeles	16%
Stanford University	15%
City University of New York	14%
Texas Southern University	14%
University of Miami	14%
University of Southwestern Louisiana	14%
George Washington University	13%
Harvard University	13%
Miami-Dade Community College	12%
University of Pennsylvania	12%
University of Southern California	12%

SOURCE: Institute of International Education, New York City.

COLLEGES PRODUCING THE MOST PH.D.S PER CAPITA

1. Harvey Mudd College
2. California Institute of Technology
3. Reed College
4. University of Chicago
5. Massachusetts Institute of Technology
6. Swarthmore College
7. Haverford College
8. Oberlin College
9. Harvard University
10. New College of the University of South Florida
11. University of California at San Diego
12. Amherst College
13. Carleton College
14. Cooper Union
15. Pomona College

SOURCE: "An Analysis of Leading Undergraduate Sources of Ph.D.s Adjusted for Institutional Size." Cited in *Ph.D. Recipients,* by Carol H. Fuller, The Great Lakes College Association. Cited in *Change* magazine, November/December 1986.

COLLEGES PRODUCING THE MOST BLACK PH.D.S

Talladega College, Alabama
Morehouse College, Georgia
Spelman College, Georgia
Tougaloo College, Mississippi
Clark College, Georgia
Fisk University, Tennessee
Dillard University, Louisiana
Xavier University, Louisiana
Virginia State University, Virginia
Morgan State University, Maryland

SOURCE: Survey by Marian Brazziel Associates under contract from the National Endowment for the Humanities. Based on a study of a five-year period, 1975–80.

SCHOOLS PRODUCING THE MOST TOP-LEVEL BUSINESS EXECUTIVES

1. Yale University
2. City University of New York

3. Harvard University
4. Princeton University
5. University of Wisconsin
6. University of California
7. New York University
8. University of Michigan
9. University of Pennsylvania
10. University of Illinois
11. University of North Carolina
12. University of Minnesota

SOURCE: *Standard and Poor's 1987 Executive/College Survey.* The list is drawn from personal data submitted by 70,000 executives. Approximately 32,000 of those who submitted data are presidents or vice presidents of corporations, while the rest hold a variety of other senior positions.

SCHOOLS PRODUCING THE MOST TOP-LEVEL BUSINESS EXECUTIVES PER CAPITA

1. Yale University
2. Princeton University
3. Harvard University
4. Dartmouth College
5. Williams College
6. Amherst College
7. Massachusetts Institute of Technology
8. Washington and Lee University
9. California Institute of Technology
10. Cornell University
11. Columbia University
12. University of Pennsylvania
13. University of Chicago
14. The Johns Hopkins University
15. Illinois Institute of Technology

SOURCE: *Standard and Poor's 1985 Executive Survey.* Per capita adjustment of Standard and Poor's data supplied by R. Stephen Richards, associate professor of psychology at Virginia Military Institute.

MOST ALUMNI IN THE 100TH CONGRESS

Yale University   (20)
Harvard University   (16)

University of Texas at Austin   (11)
University of California at Los Angeles   (9)
University of Florida   (8)
Princeton University   (7)
Stanford University   (7)
University of Alabama   (6)
Georgetown University   (6)
University of North Carolina at Chapel Hill   (5)
University of Notre Dame   (5)
Ohio State University   (5)
University of Pittsburgh   (5)
Syracuse University   (5)
Willamette University   (5)
University of Wisconsin at Madison   (5)

SOURCE: *1987 Congressional Staff Directory.*

UNIVERSITIES THAT GET THE MOST MONEY FROM ALUMNI

	1985–86 Total
1. Harvard University	$55,243,934
2. Stanford University	$54,537,291
3. Yale University	$53,616,922
4. Cornell University	$43,530,518
5. Princeton University	$42,492,560
6. Texas A&M University	$24,983,421
7. Dartmouth College	$22,609,718
8. Columbia University	$22,292,378
9. Vanderbilt University	$21,677,781
10. University of Michigan	$20,511,963

SOURCE: *Survey of Voluntary Support for Education, 1985–86,* published by the Council for Aid to Education, Inc. The figures are the total dollar amounts given by alumni in 1985–86.

COLLEGES WITH THE MOST LOYAL ALUMNI

1. Swarthmore College
2. Centre College
3. Pan-American University
4. University of California at Riverside
5. Emmanuel College
6. Alfred University

7. Webb Institute of Naval Architecture
8. Williams College
9. Hamilton College
10. Hampden-Sydney College

SOURCE: *Survey of Voluntary Support for Education, 1985–86,* published by the Council for Aid to Education, Inc. The schools listed are those with the highest percentage of alumni who made donations during 1985–86.

THE MOST EXPENSIVE COLLEGES: PRIVATE

1. Bennington College
2. Sarah Lawrence College
3. Barnard College
4. University of Chicago
5. Columbia University
6. Harvard University
7. Dartmouth College
8. Tufts University
9. Yale University
10. Massachusetts Institute of Technology

SOURCE: The College Board; cited in *The Chronicle of Higher Education,* August 12, 1987.

THE MOST EXPENSIVE COLLEGES: PUBLIC

1. Colorado School of Mines   ($6,724)
2. University of California at San Diego   ($6,464)
3. University of Rhode Island   ($6,027)
4. University of Illinois at Chicago   ($5,934)
5. George Mason University   ($5,892)
6. Maine Maritime Academy   ($5,875)
7. St. Mary's College of Maryland   ($5,870)
8. University of California at Berkeley   ($5,858)
9. Lyndon State College   ($5,790)

NOTE: A tenth school in the original list, Virginia Military Institute, was deleted because expenses include uniforms and other necessities.

SOURCE: The College Board; cited in *The Chronicle of Higher Education,* August 12, 1987. Figures include in-state tuition, room and board, and fees for the 1987–88 academic year.

THE LEAST EXPENSIVE COLLEGES: PRIVATE

1. Alice Lloyd College ($2,030)
2. Berea College ($2,175)
3. Central Baptist College ($2,550)
4. Southeastern Baptist College ($3,200)
5. Wesley College ($3,300)
6. Selma University ($3,350)
7. Eastern Christian College ($3,360)
8. Arkansas Baptist College ($3,370)
9. Roanoke Bible College ($3,383)
10. Central Christian College ($3,440)

SOURCE: The College Board; cited in *The Chronicle of Higher Education,* August 12, 1987. Figures include tuition, room and board, and fees for the 1987–88 academic year.

THE LEAST EXPENSIVE COLLEGES: PUBLIC

1. Henderson State University ($2,572)
2. Alabama State University ($2,664)
3. Middle Tennessee State University ($2,698)
4. University of Arkansas at Monticello ($2,770)
5. Minot State University ($2,772)
6. Western Carolina University ($2,774)
7. University of Puerto Rico, Rio Piedras ($2,780)
8. Missouri Southern State University ($2,846)
9. Jacksonville State University ($2,873)
10. Midwestern State University ($2,922)

SOURCE: The College Board; cited in *The Chronicle of Higher Education,* August 12, 1987. Figures include in-state tuition, room and board, and fees for the 1987–88 academic year.

THE 10 LARGEST AMERICAN UNIVERSITIES (SINGLE CAM-PUSES)

Ohio State University (58,400)
University of Texas at Austin (47,600)
University of Minnesota at Twin Cities (46,400)

University of Wisconsin at Madison (42,200)
Arizona State University (40,600)
Michigan State University (40,300)
University of Maryland at College Park (38,300)
Texas A&M University (36,800)
University of Cincinnati (36,500)
University of Illinois at Champaign-Urbana (34,600)

SOURCE: *Selective Guide to Colleges,* 3rd edition, 1985.

BEST TINY COLLEGES

College of the Atlantic
Deep Springs College
Marlboro College
New College of the University of South Florida
New School for Social Research/Eugene Lang College
St. John's College, Maryland and New Mexico
Thomas Aquinas College

NOTE: All colleges listed enroll fewer than 500 students.

THE OLDEST AMERICAN COLLEGES

Harvard University	(1636)
College of William and Mary	(1693)
St. John's College, Maryland	(1696)
Yale University	(1701)
University of Pennsylvania	(1740)
Moravian College	(1742)
Princeton University	(1746)
Washington and Lee University	(1749)
Columbia University	(1754)
Brown University	(1764)
Rutgers University	(1766)
Dartmouth College	(1769)
College of Charleston	(1770)
Salem College, North Carolina	(1772)
Dickinson College	(1773)
Hampden-Sydney College	(1776)

THE NEWEST SELECTIVE COLLEGES

College of the Atlantic, Maine	(1976)
SUNY College at Purchase	(1976)
Evergreen State College, Washington	(1974)
Hampshire College, Massachusetts	(1974)
Oral Roberts University, Oklahoma	(1971)
St. John's College, New Mexico	(1969)
University of California at Irvine	(1965)
University of California at Santa Cruz	(1965)
CUNY John Jay College of Criminal Justice	(1965)
Marlboro College, Vermont	(1965)
Pitzer College, California	(1965)
University of California at San Diego	(1964)
Florida Institute of Technology	(1964)
University of Dallas	(1963)
Eckerd College, Florida	(1963)

SOURCE: Regional accrediting associations. Colleges listed according to the date they received accreditation from regional associations.

COLLEGES THAT ACCEPT THE SMALLEST PERCENTAGE OF APPLICANTS*

U.S. Coast Guard Academy	8%
U.S. Military Academy	10%
U.S. Naval Academy	11%
Stanford University	15%
Cooper Union	16%
Harvard University	16%
Princeton University	16%
U.S. Air Force Academy	16%
Duke University	18%
Yale University	18%

*Not every four-year institution provided the College Board with information on the number of freshmen accepted.

SOURCE: The College Board's Annual Survey of Colleges, 1987.

MAJOR WOMEN'S COLLEGES

Agnes Scott College
Barnard College
Bryn Mawr College
Mount Holyoke College
Randolph-Macon Woman's College
Scripps College
Smith College
Spelman College
Wellesley College

MAJOR NON-MILITARY ALL-MALE COLLEGES

Deep Springs College
Hampden-Sydney College
Morehouse College
Rose-Hulman Institute of Technology
St. John's University, Minnesota
Wabash College

THE "PUBLIC IVYS"

University of California system
Miami University of Ohio
University of Michigan at Ann Arbor
University of North Carolina at Chapel Hill
University of Texas at Austin
University of Vermont
University of Virginia
College of William and Mary

SOURCE: Richard Moll, *The Public Ivys: A Guide to America's Best Public, Undergraduate Colleges and Universities.* The Ivy League of American public universities (a.k.a. "Public Ivys") was created by Moll in his book describing the most selective and academically competitive public schools in the country.

COLLEGES WITH NAMES MOST OFTEN CONFUSED

Cornell University, New York, and Cornell College, Iowa
Cornell College, Iowa, and Grinnell College, Iowa
DePauw University, Indiana, and DePaul University, Illinois

University of Miami, Florida, and Miami University, Ohio

City University of New York, New York, and New York University, New York

St. John's College, Maryland and New Mexico, St. John's University, Minnesota, and St. John's University, New York

Trinity College, Connecticut, Trinity College, Washington, D.C., and Trinity University, Texas

Washington University, Missouri, and the University of Washington, Washington

Wellesley College, Massachusetts, and Wesleyan University, Connecticut

Williams College, Massachusetts, and the College of William and Mary, Virginia

THE HOTTEST RIVALRIES

University of Alabama vs. Auburn University

Amherst College vs. Williams College

University of California at Berkeley vs. Stanford University

University of California at Los Angeles vs. University of Southern California

Duke University vs. University of North Carolina at Chapel Hill

University of Georgia vs. Georgia Institute of Technology

Hampden-Sydney College vs. Washington and Lee University

Harvard University vs. Yale University

Lafayette College vs. Lehigh University

University of Michigan vs. Ohio State University

University of Nebraska vs. University of Oklahoma

SCHOOLS WITH NAMES MOST OFTEN MISSPELLED

Centre College

Duquesne University

Fairleigh Dickinson University

Marquette University

Rensselaer Polytechnic Institute
Wellesley College
Worcester Polytechnic Institute

COLLEGES WITH BETTER-KNOWN ACRONYMS THAN NAMES

MIT—Massachusetts Institute of Technology
NYU—New York University
RPI—Rensselaer Polytechnic Institute
SMU—Southern Methodist University
TCU—Texas Christian University
UCLA—University of California at Los Angeles
UNLV—University of Nevada at Las Vegas
USC—University of Southern California
UVA—University of Virginia
UVM—University of Vermont
VMI—Virginia Military Institute
W & L—Washington and Lee University

COLLEGES OFFERING UNUSUAL MAJORS

Film Animation
Columbia College, Illinois
University of Toledo

Fluids and Plasmas
Massachusetts Institute of Technology

Funeral Services
Indiana Central University
Wayne State College, Nebraska

Holography
Hampshire College, Massachusetts

International/Comparative Home Economics
Friends World College, New York
Indiana State University

Interpreter for the Deaf

Bloomburg University of Pennsylvania
Eastern Kentucky University
Maryville College, Tennessee

Iranian Languages

University of Texas at Austin

Mycology

Friends World College, New York
State University of New York—College of Environmental Science and Forestry at Syracuse
University of Texas at Austin

Ophthalmic Services

Colby-Sawyer College, New Hampshire

Psycholinguistics

Massachusetts Institute of Technology
University of Massachusetts at Amherst

Yiddish

City University of New York, Queens
Friends World College, New York

SOURCE: The Index of Majors, The College Entrance Examination Board.

COLLEGES WITH THE MOST COMPREHENSIVE STUDY-ABROAD PROGRAMS

Dartmouth College
Goshen College
Earlham College
Friends World College, New York
Kalamazoo College
Lewis and Clark College
University of Massachusetts at Amherst
Macalester College

Middlebury College
St. Olaf College
Stanford University

SOURCE: Council on International Educational Exchange and foreign study departments at various colleges.

COLLEGES WHERE PHI BETA KAPPA CHAPTERS HAVE BEEN CHARTERED SINCE 1980

Alma College (1980)
Claremont McKenna College (1983)
Drew University (1980)
Luther College (1983)
University of Miami (1983)
Villanova University (1986)
Western Maryland College (1980)

SOURCE: Phi Beta Kappa

COLLEGES WITH UNUSUAL MASCOTS

University of California at Irvine	Anteaters
Colby College	White Mules
Colorado School of Mines	Orediggers
Evergreen State College	Geoducks
Furman College	Paladins
Georgetown University	Hoyas
Georgia Institute of Technology	Ramblin' Wreck
University of Maryland	Terrapins
University of North Carolina at Chapel Hill	Tar Heels
Oberlin College	Yeomen
Pepperdine University	Waves
Pomona-Pitzer Colleges	Sage Hens
Presbyterian College	Blue Hose
Rollins College	Tars
Stetson University	Hatters
Texas Christian University	Horned Frogs

Tufts University	Jumbos
Virginia Polytechnic Institute and State University	Hokies
Yeshiva University	Maccabees

UNUSUAL SPORTS TEAMS AT SELECTIVE COLLEGES

CANOEING:

University of the South

CRICKET:

Emory University
Haverford College

FIGURE SKATING:

Harvard University
Miami University

FLYING:

Carnegie-Mellon University
University of Illinois at Champaign-Urbana
Kenyon College
Ohio University
Oklahoma State University
University of Oklahoma
Rose-Hulman Institute of Technology

HANDBALL:

Lake Forest College
Miami University

PING-PONG:

Loyola University

POLO:

University of Connecticut
Cornell University
New York University
Skidmore College
University of Virginia

RACQUETBALL:
Loyola University, California
Loyola University, Illinois
Miami University
University of Puget Sound

RODEO:
University of Missouri

SCUBA:
Columbia University
Evergreen State College
Virginia Military Institute

TRAP AND SKEET:
University of Cincinnati
Southern Methodist University

WATER SKIING:
Eckerd College
Rollins College

COLLEGES WITH THE MOST MEN'S SPORTS TEAMS

Massachusetts Institute of Technology	22
Harvard University	20
Amherst College	17
University of California at San Diego	17
Cornell University	17
Dartmouth College	17
Yale University	17
Brown University	15

SOURCE: *The National Directory of College Athletics,* Ray Franks Publishing Ranch, Amarillo, Texas 79109.

WINNERS OF THE MOST NCAA DIVISION I CHAMPIONSHIPS—WOMEN'S SPORTS

University of Southern California	Basketball
Old Dominion University	Field hockey
University of Florida	Golf

University of Utah	Gymnastics
University of North Carolina	Soccer
University of California at Los Angeles	Softball
Stanford University	Tennis
University of the Pacific	Volleyball

SOURCE: *The National Directory of College Athletics,* Roy Franks Publishing Ranch, Amarillo, Texas 79109.

COLLEGES WITH THE BEST COLLEGE NEWSPAPERS

The Auburn Plainsman, Auburn University
The Daily Texan, University of Texas at Austin
Falcon Times, Miami-Dade Community College
The Graphic, Pepperdine University
The MATC Times, Milwaukee Area Technical College
The Ranger, San Antonio College
The State News, Michigan State University
Valley Star, Los Angeles Valley College

SOURCE: Associated Collegiate Press, Minneapolis, Minnesota. These college papers have been the most frequent winners of the Associated Collegiate Press Pacemakers Award since 1961.

COLLEGES WITH THE BEST DEBATE TEAMS

Brigham Young University
University of California at Berkeley
University of California at Los Angeles
California State University at Long Beach
California State University at Northridge
University of Southern Colorado
Southern Illinois University at Carbondale
United States Air Force Academy
Wheaton College, Illinois
University of Wyoming

SOURCE: Cross-Examination Debate Association. Debate teams from these colleges have earned the most total points in the Cross-Examination Debate Association's annual sweepstakes since the competition began in 1971.

SELECTIVE COLLEGES WITH BAGPIPE BANDS

Alma College
The Citadel
College of William and Mary
Macalester College
U.S. Military Academy
University of Iowa
Williams College

SCHOOLS ORGANIZED AROUND RESIDENTIAL COLLEGES OR HOUSES*

University of California at Santa Cruz
Harvard University
University of Miami
Northwestern University
Princeton University
Rice University
Smith College
Yale University

*Residential colleges or houses are defined as living/learning units where students live, work and socialize with affiliated faculty members.

UNIVERSITIES WITH THE BIGGEST LIBRARIES

1. Harvard University	11.0 million volumes
2. Yale University	8.1 million volumes
3. University of Illinois at Champaign-Urbana	7.0 million volumes
4. University of California at Berkeley	6.8 million volumes
5. University of Michigan at Ann Arbor	6.0 million volumes
6. Columbia University	5.5 million volumes
7. University of Texas at Austin	5.5 million volumes
8. University of California at Los Angeles	5.4 million volumes

9. Stanford University	5.4 million volumes
10. Cornell University	4.8 million volumes

SOURCE: Association of Research Library Statistics, 1985–86.

UNIVERSITIES THAT SPEND THE MOST ON RESEARCH

The Johns Hopkins University	$388,553,000
Massachusetts Institute of Technology	$242,966,000
University of Wisconsin at Madison	$208,425,000
Cornell University	$203,226,000
Stanford University	$199,185,000
University of Minnesota	$173,322,000
University of Washington	$163,962,000
University of Michigan	$163,713,000
University of California at Berkeley	$149,900,000
University of California at Los Angeles	$149,744,000

SOURCE: National Science Foundation, as quoted in *The Chronicle of Higher Education,* December 10, 1986. The figures are for fiscal 1985 and represent the total spent from funds supplied by government, industry and the university itself.

UNIVERSITIES WITH THE LARGEST ENDOWMENTS

1. Harvard University	$3.4 billion
2. University of Texas system	$2.5 billion
3. Princeton University	$1.9 billion
4. Yale University	$1.7 billion
5. Stanford University	$1.4 billion
6. Texas A&M University	$1.3 billion
7. Columbia University	$1.1 billion
8. Massachusetts Institute of Technology	$970 million
9. Washington University, Missouri	$960 million
10. University of Chicago	$800 million

SOURCE: *The Chronicle of Higher Education,* May 20, 1987.

SCHOOLS WITH THE LARGEST ENDOWMENT PER STUDENT

Private	*Public*
Princeton University	Virginia Military Institute
Harvard University	University of Virginia
California Institute	University of Delaware
of Technology	University of Cincinnati
Rice University	College of William and Mary
Swarthmore College	University of Pittsburgh
Grinnell College	

SOURCE: *The Chronicle of Higher Education,* May 20, 1987. Both graduate and undergraduate students are included in the per capita total.